Chakras and Auras: A Practical Guide to Your Energetic Body

~ *Friend to Friend Series* ~

Mary Shannon

"The most difficult task with which we are presented is to maintain and bring forth love on a daily basis through all our life experiences. This, my friend, is the main impetus for returning to our school called Earth"

James Van Praagh ~*The Power of Love*

Copyright© 2018 by Mary Shannon

All rights reserved. No portion of this book may be reproduced - mechanically, electronically, or by any other means including photocopy - without written permission of the publisher.

www.sevencupsmystic.com

For my soul family, Dave and Molly, thank you for incarnating with me

~ Friend to Friend Series ~

My goal in these books is to act as your friend in explaining spiritual and esoteric topics in a way that is down to earth and practical for your everyday life. I want my best friend to read this series and gain a better understanding of the metaphysical world. In the same vein, I hope that you find these books entertaining and educational. My desire is that you can learn in a fun environment and then spread this knowledge out to your own friend base. This way we can all benefit from this knowledge that should be a part of our everyday education.

CONTENTS

Introduction 1

Chakra Basics 7

What is a chakra? 7
The Seven Main Chakras 8
The "Other" Chakras 27
Chakra States 31

Aura Basics 39

What is an aura? 39
Aura Colors 41
Aura Conditions 52

Energy Basics 57

What Does Energy Feel like? 57
What Does Energy Look like? 60
What Does Energy Sound like? 62

Discovering your Energetic Body 65

How to See your Chakras and Aura 66
How to Feel your Chakras and Aura 71

How to Hear your Chakras and Aura	73
How to Know about your Chakras and Aura	74
The Pendulum Method	75

Balancing your Energetic Body   81

The Power of Thought	82
Vibrational Healing	85
Specific Chakra Healing	89
Yoga	89
Meditation	90
Protective bubble	94
Energy Healing	96

Chakra and Aura Activities   99

What Kind of Aura…	99
Painting Rooms	103
The Story of You	105

Conclusion   111

Meditations   113

Cord cutting meditation	113
Meditations for each chakra	115
Full Chakra cleaning and spinning meditation	123
My Personal Daily Meditation	126

Introduction

I want to start off this book by explaining where I come from when I speak of chakras and auras. What type of friend is this that is explaining the chakra system to you? Know your source - right.

First, let's start by defining who I am not. I am not your advanced yogini friend. I am not going to explain to you the importance of your root chakra while in warrior one. Along these same lines, I am not going to tell you the "traditional" name for these chakras or their corresponding sounds. That is just not the type of friend I am.

I am coming at this topic from a Western perspective. I have not had extensive training in the ancient eastern traditions and my yoga habit does not extend beyond regular class attendance. My culture has influenced my perceptions and you should know that about my associations with different colors and thoughts. I am, at my core, a Western practitioner.

Instead of the advanced eastern practitioner sitting in full lotus position - it is me - your buddy Mary Shannon who is that quirky psychic friend. You know, the one that will tell you when you are just not grounded or when your aura just seems a little "off". I am coming to you from the position of observing the energy of my clients, friends, family and even myself over the years. I have used my third-eye to "see" these chakras and auras and I have felt whether they are "off" or a little "icky". I use this information to benefit my own life and those that I interact with - so that everyone can live a balanced and harmonious existence.

So, what does all this mean? How does someone use this information to help them in real world non-woo-woo ways? For me, personally, this takes the form of watching my chakras and aura closely so that I can balance and heal any issues that come up before the energetic blocks affect my physical body. I pay close attention to my root and heart chakras - knowing that these chakras close easily for me and can get "gunked up" with energy blocks if I am not paying attention. I know that if I have a hole in my aura, 75% of the time it is either going to be near my heart or at the bottom of my feet. By following my energy system, I can spot problems and fix them before they get too advanced.

As an example of how I use this knowledge, I had an experience not too long ago when I let fear get the better of me and felt my energy close up and the potential for blocks form. It all started one spooky Friday night - imagine a heavy fog blanketing a quiet forest. Well...that may be a little exaggerated. It was really just a chill Friday night when I made some decisions that led my chakras to not be too happy with me.

The energy shift had begun earlier in the evening when I had taken some pain medication to relieve a headache that had plagued me all day and my energy defenses were down. Combine that with the hubby being gone late at his monthly poker outing and I was setting myself up for energy crisis. All it took was staying up past my usual ten pm bedtime listening to a scary thriller audiobook and I pretty much set myself up for a sleepless night. As I was trying to fall asleep I could actually feel a heaviness and sensation of fear and anxiety settle over my heart area.

When I woke up the next morning I felt "off" - I knew that my chakras and aura were not functioning at their top level. Luckily this was a Saturday which meant no client readings - I was not in a state to connect for other people.

So, what did my energy look like? My root chakra (and my sub-chakras - more on those later) had all closed up and there was a black energy block covering the area of my heart in my aura. Eeek! What is a psychic to do with an energy system like this?!

I focused on that heart block and clearing that energy while grounding my system. Yeah - totally woo-woo speak there - so what does that actually mean? I took some time in the morning to meditate, for me that particular morning my meditation practice took the form of journaling my thoughts and feelings - yes, journaling can count as a meditative practice. I could tell I was disappointed in myself for letting fear take hold - I should have used my knowledge of different energy techniques to kick this in the butt the night before instead of letting it get this far. I find some of the best medicine is to be honest with yourself and your feelings.

Later in the day (I'm a busy wife and mom, there is only so much that can be done before the sun rises) I did some restorative yoga poses focusing on opening my heart. While in these poses I listening to a heart chakra binaural beats meditation I found off YouTube. I also gave myself some Reiki (healing energy) during this time and put my large black tourmaline crystal at my feet to pull out any negativity and ground my energy. Then I read an uplifting book focused on the energy of love (*The*

Power of Love by James Van Praagh) - putting a moratorium on anything "scary".

By taking the time to look at my energy and fix it before it went any further downhill, I was able to shift my mood and energy system. Even my non-woo woo husband could tell that my energy was "off" and appreciated the change that came when I had cleared the energy blocks and opened my chakras. But let me be honest here, the energy system can close down quickly but sometimes takes a while to heal. This was not a one-day process. My root chakra took a few days to become fully back on track and functioning properly.

This is what I want to accomplish with this book - I want you to be able to pay attention to your chakras and aura and notice when there is something "wrong" or amiss with them. I want to give you the tools and techniques to fix these issues or at least start you down the path for that to occur (sometimes a qualified energy healer is what is really needed).

To accomplish this, first, we will start out focusing on your chakras - what they are and how they work. Then we will do the same things with your aura - a discussion of what an aura is and a description of what the different colors can mean. I have combined both these systems into one book because they function together beautifully. When one chakra is closed or not functioning properly, you will sometimes see a corresponding block or disturbance in the auric field. The energy system all works together.

Following this introductory material, I will give you some basics on what this thing called energy really looks and feels like. You will need this information as we then discuss some different methods you can use to determine if your chakras are functioning properly and what your aura looks like. Once you figure out what you need to work on, we will then look at different ways to balance those chakras and cleanse that aura. Finally, we will end with a little fun, examining some ways to incorporate all this new knowledge into your daily life.

All I ask of you is to sit back, relax and keep your mind open.

Chakra Basics

What is a chakra?

You may have heard the term bantered around throughout your daily life - "your chakras are out of balance", "that dude needs to realign his chakra", "this will be good for your root chakra". Wherever you have heard about them, whether from yoga class or your local health food store, you likely know that chakras are important. But what are they exactly?

Basically, chakras are energy centers that we all have throughout our body. There are the traditional seven major chakras and then there are countless other "minor" chakras throughout our body and even below and above our physical bodies.

The seven major chakras are seen by some as the most important and likely what you have heard the most about. These chakras are located up your spine, from the base all the way to the tip of your head. There are colors and numbers and fancy names, and all sorts of different things associated with each of these chakras. Taping into these corresponding influences can help you to balance or open or unblock these centers.

So, what exactly does it mean when I say "energy center"? Let's break this down a little more. We are all made of energy, even mainstream science can agree on that. This energy vibrates at different frequencies and has different effects on each of us. Chakras are places in your body where different frequencies of vibrations collect. They are essentially little pools or reservoirs in your body where certain energy vibrations are the most prominent. When they are all in balanced and aligned it helps our body and our mind to feel great and function properly. When one of these centers is out of balance the energy does not flow smoothly from our feet to our head and this can cause us to feel a little out of sorts.

The Seven Main Chakras

We are going to start our discussion of the specific chakras in the body by focusing on the seven main ones. These are the most popular for a reason - they are the biggest and tend to have the greatest influence on our lives. These are the vibrations that we encounter and experience every day, some more than others, but they are common in our society.

The Root Chakra...not your Mama's Grounding

The first chakra we are going to explore is the root chakra. This is considered the first of the seven major chakras and is located at the base of the spine. This chakra is seen as a deep red swirling vortex of energy. Yep - picture a big blob of red energy where your booty connects to your chair and that is basically the root chakra.

So, what is this Root Chakra really about?

When people talk about the root chakra they generally mention its association with survival. This is the first chakra we focus on when we are infants. Think about all the things that a baby is concerned about and you will find a lot of things associated with this chakra. Basic survival needs - food, shelter, warmth, comfort, fear - that sort of thing.

The root chakra is also all about grounding or our connection to the earth and our physical reality - it is not a coincidence that the element associated with this chakra is earth. When we get all caught up "in our head" or thinking about our world instead of living in it, then this chakra can become unbalanced and out of sync.

A lot of us who are interested and focused on the metaphysical world and our connection to the spirit world may want to bypass this chakra and pay more attention to opening and balancing the third eye or crown chakras. Let's face it - this chakra can seem a little boring. But by focusing on our grounding and everyday reality, it actually helps us to form a stronger and deeper connection with our higher selves and, in turn, our spiritual team. We are incarnate on this earth for a reason - don't miss out on the actual experience by focusing on an alternate reality instead of the reality that you are meant to experience.

What is the Root of your problem?

When this chakra is out of balance or blocked you may feel flighty and have a hard time focusing on the present moment. You get that sense of being "high" and you may even bump into walls or furniture because of the lack of connection with your body. And yes, those who partake it too many substances which leave them high do tend to have closed off root chakras.

So, what does it actually look like to have an unbalanced root chakra? My sister is a great example as she went from being firmly rooted to having her root chakra out of "whack".

When she was growing up, my sister was a great soccer player. One of those that play year-round in a variety of leagues - both indoor and outdoor. During this time, she had the most amazing memory (exercise is a great grounding technique) and would regularly correct us on what "really" happened two or four or ten years ago.

Now it is a different story. Instead of playing soccer year-round she is the mother of three young children (three under 5 years of age). She has trouble finding time for any self-care and her great memory has dissolved, especially her short-term memory. She spends most of her day "in her head" planning the future - dinner, naps, how to get that marker stain out of the couch cushion. This day to day reality does not help out her root chakra which has become closed and blocked because of the anxiety and busyness of raising small children.

Balancing that Root

There are a lot of different ways to balance your chakras in general which we will look at in depth later, but, for this chakra, grounding is my favorite method. Grounding involves activities that get you back in your body like exercise or connecting with the ground. Many people (myself included) enjoy stepping onto grass in bare feet to let the energy from your body flow into the ground and bring up the stable, calming energy of the earth. I know, sounds a little silly, but try it, you may find you enjoy it. I tend to do this in the morning while letting the dog out to use the bathroom (but not in the winter, I'm not a masochist!). I just step in a spot I know he doesn't tinkle and let the energy flow while enjoying the beauty of the outdoors.

If my sister was asking me how to get her root chakra back open again, I would likely advise that she takes a little time for herself each week to engage in heavy and strenuous exercise. Her energy body was used to this kind of physical activity as she was growing up and likely became accustomed to it. Now, for me, I was never super physically active (even though I was at one time co-captain of my high school's tennis team). So, personally, the type of physical activity my body craves is walks through the woods to ground my energy.

Crystals are also great for working with chakras and the ones associated with this chakra are those that are red, brown or black in color. My favorite crystals to work with for the root chakra are ruby, red jasper, and black tourmaline. Ruby provides an intense feminine power that is very grounding and stable while red jasper offers a lighter, less harsh vibration that is similar to rubies. Black tourmaline is a powerful stone that provides both energetic protection and grounding. I keep a large chunk of it underneath the desk I do my readings at to ground my energy and keep me connected to this world.

Some people even like to use petrified wood or stones from the ground to align this chakra. Anything connected to the earth will greatly assist in balancing this chakra.

The Sacral Chakra...aka the Fun Zone

The sacral chakra is the second of the seven major chakras and is located just below your belly button. This chakra vibrates at the orange color frequency. When you look at the color orange how do you feel? When you see someone out in public wearing orange what kind of judgments do you immediately make about them? Are they fun-loving spirits or just fashion challenged?

This sacral chakra is also associated with the element of water. Think about all the different states that water can be in. When you add heat, it starts to boil. But when water is cold it is frozen in place. Do your hips move to the beat and flow like water or are they stiff as a board and frozen like ice?

Astrological 5th House - Fun, Creativity and Sex

So why do I call this chakra "the fun zone"? This chakra is all about fun and creativity. When it is functioning properly you will be living your life with enjoyment in your heart and finding that "sunny side of the street".

Along with fun, this chakra is also the seat of our creativity. Those creative urges you have, likely come from this point. If you are at all interested in astrology, I like to think of this chakra as similar to the 5th House. Those aspects that are associated with the 5th House are normally associated with the sacral chakra as well.

Now, what else is that 5th House associated with? Sex and babies. Look where this chakra is located - right by your reproductive organs. Makes sense now doesn't it! This swirling vortex of light right over those organs can tell us a lot about the state of that area in your life.

Debbie Downer - Blocked or Closed Sacral Chakra

When the sacral chakra is out of balance or blocked you may feel like you are stuck in the same boring day to day routine. Life will just seem blah and grey and you won't get much enjoyment out of it. This is that feeling some people get in the middle of winter where they can't stand another grey day. Think of that grey day as a blocked sacral chakra. It just needs some bright shiny orange light to make it smile again.

Other signs that this chakra is not functioning up to par are a lackluster sex life or difficulty getting or staying pregnant. Sometimes you will see this chakra represented as a frozen ice cube when there is not enough heat and passion there to thaw it out. Trouble with creativity and writer's block can also be symptoms of a non-functioning chakra.

Because of the average age of my clients, I end up getting a fair amount of questions regarding trouble conceiving a child. When I check the energy system of these women, nine times out of ten their sacral chakra will be closed or blocked. I was privy to watch one close friend go from many infertility troubles and a very closed sacral chakra to an open chakra and a brand new baby. Needless to say, this chakra is important in the baby making process.

Opening the Doors to Fun

Now with all the things this chakra is associated with, you may be wondering how to get yours functioning to the highest degree possible. An easy way to help open and balance this chakra is to do something fun! Dance like no one is watching or go to a movie on a weekday or paint a picture. Do something that makes you giddy as a child. The idea is to bring passion into your life and get that water moving freely and not frozen stiff.

Those crystal vibrations associated with this chakra are the color orange. My favorites include orange calcite and carnelian. Orange calcite has a gentle calm vibration that will ease you into your creativity. Carnelian is more intense and has the energy of a master's in art student wrapped up in completing their thesis masterpiece.

Wearing the color orange can also help you to raise the vibrations of this chakra. Try adding orange to your life in fun and creative ways - what about painting your fingernails orange so that every time you look at them you can remember that life is all about fun!

The Solar Plexus Chakra...Let Your Light Shine

The solar plexus - likely you have heard this term used at some point in your life (maybe in gym class?), so you may have a vague idea about where this energy center is located. To be a little more specific, this third chakra is located about two finger widths above your belly button. This chakra's color is yellow - think bright sunshiny thoughts - that kind of beautiful yellow color.

And just like the sun, this chakra corresponds to the element of fire. This is where those passionate fires burn inside of you. This is also the place that gets you going and "puts a fire under you" to get you to work towards your goals.

Confidence and Willpower - Open Solar Plexus Chakra

Now think about how yellow makes you feel. When you see someone wearing a bright yellow shirt do you think "wow they must have some confidence to pull off that shirt"? Well, this chakra is all about confidence. When your solar plexus is open and functioning properly you won't have to take twenty minutes to decide what outfit to wear in the morning, you will be able to make decisions quickly because you know what you like - and it doesn't really matter what other people think.

This solar plexus chakra is the center where your ego and identity lies. If you feel secure in who you are and how you describe yourself, you will stand up tall and walk with pride. All these feelings come from that stomach area - that solar plexus.

A healthy solar plexus chakra will also be reflected in someone who is a "go-getter" and does not need a lot of outside motivation or stimulus to do their work. They will have personal discipline and know when to put down that second/third cookie.

Indecisive, Shy and Sluggish - Closed or Blocked Solar Plexus Chakra

Now if you try on 50 outfits before finally flinging on a black t-shirt and jeans in the morning you might have a blocked chakra - or you might just really like wearing black and being comfortable. People whose third chakras are closed or blocked may have a difficult time taking initiative and making decisions.

The individual who is overly shy and has a difficult time interacting with other people may have an unbalanced solar plexus chakra as well. Usually, this stems from a lack of confidence in who they are and why they are here, and this will reflect in the energy of their solar plexus. You may even visually see someone with a closed solar plexus using their arms to shield this area when meeting other people - think of where you cross your arms in front of you when you feel uncomfortable.

Another trait of someone whose solar plexus chakra is not functioning to the highest potential is that they may appear sluggish and like they lack energy. They just don't have that "fire" in their belly to get them up and doing. Instead, they may sit and binge watch Netflix all weekend - but, of course, I'm not saying that everyone who binge watches Netflix has a blocked solar plexus (but if you do this too often it may cause your solar plexus to start to close...lesson learned here)!

I have also frequently seen this chakra be overactive, especially in men. This is not a gender stereotype, more of a comment on our societal structure as it currently stands. Some men are too confident, their ego (and sometimes their waistline in this area) are inflated. That domineering boss that just won't let up - yep, he may have an overactive solar plexus chakra.

How Do I Decide What to Wear - Balancing that Solar Plexus Chakra

To get this chakra back in balance my best advice is to "fake it until you make it". Pretend you have the confidence you want to have. Tell yourself you are worth it and you can achieve anything you put your mind to. There is a lot of research behind this idea of pretending to be one way to actually assume those qualities.

I've got a story on this one as I used to have a pretty closed solar plexus chakra, especially in those awkward teenage years when you just don't know who you are or who you want to be. I used to be one of those shy kids who sits there terrified that the teacher will call on you, not wanting to speak in front of all my classmates. What if I said something stupid - the ridicule of high school kids can be cruel. But then, one day I decided that I didn't want to be that way anymore.

I was tired of living with a closed solar plexus chakra (although, I didn't really know about chakras back then). So one day while I was sitting in Sophomore English class I thought - nope, not going to do this anymore. I decided that I needed to be more confident in who I was and my knowledge, therefore, I was going to challenge myself to raise my hand at least two times in that class every day. Yep, I was going to stand proudly as the nerd I was and try for some of those class participation points. I kept this up, eventually challenging myself in more and more classes and soon I became confident in myself and who I was.

So sometimes you just need to decide to be one way and then just go out and do it. Fake being confident and eventually, you will become confident.

The crystals associated with this chakra are those that are yellow (are you catching on to the pattern here - most of the time the color of the chakra corresponds to the color of the crystal). My favorite crystals to use for this chakra are citrine and tiger's eye. Citrine is a popular stone and contains a radiant energy that mirrors the sun. Tiger's eye's energy is more forceful and I like to use it when I know I am going to need to "level up" in my confidence - think big projects or confrontations.

I also like to use golden selenite, especially to find confidence in your spiritual pursuits and connection with your guides. However golden selenite is one of those stones that are not always easy to find, whereas tiger's eye and citrine are very common and are found in most metaphysical stores.

The Heart Chakra...That Loving Feeling

The heart chakra is located, guess where, by the heart! This fourth chakra resonates to the color green. And just as easy to remember, this chakra corresponds to those loving feelings you have. See - not too difficult to remember what this chakra is all about!

This chakra is also associated with healing as love is seen as the ultimate healing force. Those who practice Reiki or other energy healing methods may find that this healing energy travels first to their heart chakra before moving out through their hands or other body parts.

The Pink Chakra

Some people feel that pink is also associated with this chakra, but the pink is actually associated with a "higher heart chakra" (more on this later) which is located just above the heart chakra, between the heart and throat chakra. The pink chakra corresponds to the ideas of unconditional love and learning to love yourself.

Heart Troubles

When this chakra is unbalanced you may have a lack of empathy and have trouble loving or feeling loved. You may find yourself judging others harshly and criticizing or gossiping about other people. People with a closed heart chakra may also feel isolated and not connected to those around them - not being able to see the loving force that unites us all. Someone with a closed heart chakra may also speak negatively about themselves and have difficulty seeing the good in who they are.

It is very easy to block or close this chakra down when you are experiencing emotional drama or pain. But, this chakra is very important and one that you should be careful not to keep closed for too long.

Opening your Heart

My favorite way to get this chakra back on track is to listen to a heart-opening meditation (there are plenty of free guided meditations on the internet and I've also included one in the Meditation section in the back of this book). You can also work on expressing gratitude to yourself and to others.

And don't forget about the importance of loving yourself. Just changing the way you talk about yourself, in private and with other people, can help you open up that heart chakra. When looking at yourself in the mirror, don't focus on your perceived "faults", instead, tell yourself how wonderful you are and what a beautiful soul you have. And, why don't you work on telling everyone in your life this too, especially those children that you are around?

Crystals associated with this chakra are green in color with pink also being used to correspond with that "higher" heart chakra. Some of my favorites include rose quartz, malachite and green aventurine. Rose quartz is a light pink color and has a gentle energy of love that radiates out of it. This is a nice crystal to use on a daily basis and is a popular stone found in many stores (even some grocery stores). I like to use malachite, which is a rich green color, to bring up deep emotional issues to the surface so that you can deal with them. This is also a good stone to be around when you are going through times of transitions, especially if those transitions are emotional. Green Aventurine has a subtler effect, providing some heart chakra work while also being associated with luck.

The Throat Chakra...Can You Hear Me Now?

The throat chakra is another one whose location is easy to remember. It is located in the throat, specifically at the top of the throat right under your tongue. This chakra is a blue color, usually somewhat lighter on the color spectrum like a sky blue. The throat chakra is associated with how you communicate, both to yourself and to others.

I don't know about you, but I can be shy at times. When I know that I am going to need to talk to people in a social setting I make sure that this chakra is open and fully functioning. In our daily society, sometimes we don't use this chakra's location enough as we spend our days communicating online and in written form instead of through our voice.

Holding Back Those Words

When this chakra is blocked or closed you may have trouble speaking your truth or speaking at all. Sore throats are a common symptom of throat chakras that are out of balance. If you ever notice someone who coughs a lot or seems to clear their throat constantly, this can sometimes be associated with a blocked throat chakra. Perhaps they are holding back words that need to be spoken and those words are trying to get out! Or, of course, they may just have a cold, in that case, blame the throat clearing on that seasonal cold.

An overactive throat chakra usually presents itself as a "chatty Cathy" - someone who just doesn't know when it is right to stop talking. Gossiping and negative talk can also be associated with an out of balance throat chakra. Those stereotypical cheerleaders you see in the movies who just keep talking even after the subject of their rant has walked away - those characters likely are presenting with an overactive throat chakra.

Clearing the Throat

To realign this chakra, I love to use my voice and sing! Sing with your full voice - yep that screeching in the shower singing at the topic of your lungs voice.

And if you need to balance that sacral chakra you can combine the activities by singing and dancing at the same time. Using that voice and throat chakra will start to open it back up. And really, what could it hurt? Just turn on your favorite playlist and start grooving to the beat - at least you will give your kids or roommates something to laugh about and then that will help all your chakras!

Crystals associated with the throat chakra are blue in color - I bet you could have guessed that! My favorite crystals to work with are sodalite, lapis lazuli, and celestite. Sodalite is good when you have written communication you are doing like homework or preparing for a presentation at work. I like to carry lapis lazuli in my pocket when I know I'm going to be talking a lot as the gold bands in the deep blue help to boost that solar plexus confidence as well. Celestite, along with its cousin angelite, works wonderfully when working on communicating with higher powers and your higher self.

The Third Eye Chakra...I Can See You and I'm Not Even Looking

Ahhh, the Third Eye Chakra. This is the chakra most of us new age, hippy, spiritual, intuitive, tarot reading tribe like to talk about. We all want our third eye to be blasted open so that we can "see" what others can't. I know - so that is a pretty generalized statement. But, in all likelihood, if you are in one of these communities you have heard about this third eye chakra. So what is it all really about?

The third eye chakra is located between your eyebrows, up about an inch. Some people say that it's exact location is the pineal gland in the brain. The color of this chakra differs depending on who you are talking to and their beliefs, but it is generally either an indigo or a violet color. I personally associate this chakra with the color indigo, but either option is correct.

This chakra is thought to be the center of your intuition. This is where you will pick up your intuitive knowings and is the seat of clairvoyance. When images flash into your awareness this is the location you receive them.

Here is an example for you - think of a pink cat. Now imagine that pink cat is doing ballet and wearing a purple tutu. Could you picture that image? Where did you "see" this in your mind? That is the location of your third eye chakra.

I Can't See - Closed and Blocked Third Eyes

When this chakra is blocked or closed you may have a difficult time trusting yourself or your inner guidance. I have found that fear of psychic phenomenon to be a major cause in individuals closing this chakra. The current Western culture promotes thoughts, beliefs, and programs that encourage us to be frightened of those "entities" and energies that we cannot see.

Just think about the last scary movie you saw - what made it scary? This fear then leads individuals to close down their third eye chakras so that they won't have the opportunity to encounter any "scary spirits".

Another common reason this chakra closes, especially in industrialized societies, is because of skepticism of anything psychic or in the para-psychological field. It doesn't seem to matter what scientific experiments or the literature says, many people have deeply held beliefs that the unseen is not real. Even some major religions discredit and rebuke anything in this field. Without being open to the unknown, this chakra becomes blocked and can close over time.

I Can See Clearly Now - Open Third Eyes

Now that we know what a closed third eye chakra looks like, what really happens when we open our third eye? An open third eye chakra does not mean that you are going to start suddenly seeing ghostly apparitions out of the corner of your eye or get flashes of impending doom. There really isn't anything to be afraid of in having the energy center open.

Instead, an open third eye chakra will lead you to learn to trust yourself and your instincts more. It also allows you to start to believe in those things that you cannot explain and that you don't see. It provides an openness and a willingness to experience the world around you in new and different ways. You will be able to visualize that pink cat in its tutu perfectly without much effort.

Opening the Third Eye Chakra

If you type "how to open the third eye chakra" into google you are going to get a lot of different methods people have used over the years. Some may work for you, others may not. But, in the strict sense of opening this chakra - all you really have to do is believe. Believe in the unseen, in energy, in the spiritual process. Even just reading books by a variety of enlightened authors can help open this chakra.

Practicing visualizations including through guided meditations will also help to open this chakra. A fun, and not too spiritual way, to help strengthen this chakra is to listen to audiobooks and picture the story playing out in your head. I use this as a regular excuse to give myself some down time while still working on my psychic abilities. We all need some breaks now and then, no matter what field we are in. For me, listening to fun fictional audiobooks is both relaxing and still helps my visualization skills.

Now if you want to learn to communicate with the dead and offer your friends psychic advice, you need more than just an open third eye chakra. You need a strong and tuned in chakra and a spiritual belief system too.

Crystals associated with this chakra range in color from indigo to purple. My favorites include labradorite and iolite. Labradorite is a great stone for individuals working on strengthening their psychic senses as it provides a protective quality while allowing information and energy to flow freely. This is a popular crystal and can be found in many metaphysical stores. Many individuals also like to wear a piece of labradorite in jewelry form when performing psychic or intuitive readings. Iolite can sometimes be more difficult to find but provides an extra psychic boost with its vibrations.

The Crown Chakra...Your Wi-Fi Connection to the Divine

We have finally made it to the crown chakra - the last of the seven major chakras! This chakra is located at the top of your head. I see this chakra as violet in color, but some people see it as white. Just like with the third eye chakra, go with what resonates with you and your system - either is correct.

Like your trusted Wi-Fi connection, when this chakra is open and functioning you are connected to a divinity - a higher power - a sense of oneness with all beings. For those who are into the woo-woo, this is generally where your connection to your spirit guides, higher self, angels and loved ones on the other side comes through.

Closed Crown Chakra - Weak Signal

In our modern age, I've seen a lot of people shut down this crown chakra, sometimes due to bad experiences with organized religion and churches. Some individuals have such a sour taste due to their religious experience from childhood that they shut off all their connection to the divine. I understand this, but what people don't realize is that it disconnects them from their higher self as well.

As a test, notice what emotions you feel when you read the word God. Do you feel all warm and fuzzy? Is there a dislike or uncomfortable feeling associated with that term? Do you hold certain beliefs that disconnect you with this word? Look at your reaction and be honest with yourself.

The term God has become uncomfortable to use in our politically correct society, no matter what the context. But you know what, opening up to just that term can help open your connection with something greater. And I'm not talking about that image of God as an old man with a beard sitting in the sky. I'm talking about that divine spark inside you that connects you with something greater. I'm talking about the essence of divinity and "all that is".

So, what does this disconnection to the divine look like? A closed crown chakra may manifest as a sense of depression or despondency and can also take the physical form of headaches. You may feel like your life doesn't have any "purpose" and you are just living the daily grind one day at a time. Just a general sense of "blah".

Opening the Crown Chakra - Making the Connection

To open this chakra a daily practice of prayer or meditation, whatever form that takes for you can help. Prayer doesn't have to be what you learned in church - instead, it can take many different forms. It is simply you establishing a connection with something greater than yourself.

Crystals associated with this chakra are purple, white or clear in color. My favorites to work with are amethyst, clear quartz and selenite. Amethyst is a very popular stone that is purple. It is great to work within the dream realm as it helps stimulate your connection while in your dream state. Clear quartz is a general power stone that amps up any energy that it comes into contact with, while selenite helps to cleanse all chakras and provides a vibration of harmony with the divine.

The "Other" Chakras

Now that we have made our way through the "main" seven chakras, let us remind ourselves that those are not the only chakras we have in our body or energy system. Those seven chakras are just the ones you hear talked about the most, and that is for good reason. These seven chakras have a great effect on our body and subtle energy systems. But, now, let us take some time to talk about some of the other chakras located throughout your energy field.

Body Chakras

One of the most well-known chakras outside the core seven are the ones located on the palms of your hands. These are the chakras that you use to feel, send and receive energy. Energy healers will use these chakras to send energy to help align and heal the subtle energy bodies.

Hand chakras get exposed to a lot of everyday "wear and tear" and once you know about these chakras, you might find yourself paying closer attention to what you do with your hands throughout the day. You may also notice when you feel a need to wash your hands even though they may not necessarily be dirty - maybe it is really your energy centers that need to be cleaned!

Then there are the chakras located on the bottoms of your feet. These chakras get easily closed off with our modern society because we like to wear shoes -

particularly shoes with rubber soles which make it hard for us to feel the energy in the earth and bring that vibrational frequency into our body.

Remember the information about "earthing" or "grounding" where you step on the earth - grass not concrete - without your shoes on to re-connect with the planet and ground your energy. It is these foot chakras that you are using to push your energy out and pull energy up.

A fun little experiment I have undertaken is to go for a walk without shoes on and see how charged up you can get your foot chakras. Don't do this too often though or you will find your feet and legs aching because we have de-conditioned our feet by wearing shoes so they are not as strong as they were in centuries past when footwear wasn't such a big trend. I have also found that my foot chakras tend to close up more or even get holes in the aura over them in the winter when I am not exposing them to as much of the earth energy as usual.

We have also briefly already mentioned the "higher" heart chakra which is located just above the heart chakra and vibrates to that pink color. There are a variety of chakras similar to this around the body that are close to another chakra and have a similar resonance but a slightly higher and different frequency, like the ear chakras which are located near the throat chakra. I do not have much experience with these chakras and have not found them particularly significant in my work, but one day they may be.

Transpersonal Chakras

I have a fascination with what some new-age types call transpersonal chakras. These are the chakras located above and below the seven main chakras. If you study different systems, you will find different names and locations for each of these chakras. Some individuals claim there are five additional chakras while others say there are fourteen. Instead of giving you a full review of the theories, I will tell you what I have found to be true in my work with these chakras.

First, I have noticed that these chakras only open up when your seven main chakras are all opened and aligned. Specifically, the root and crown chakra need to be open for the chakras above and beneath your body to open as well. It feels like once the crown chakra is open then the chakra above this has the power to open and evolve as well, same with the root chakra.

In terms of numbers, you will find some individuals who say that there are seven upper and seven lower chakras that correspond with the seven main chakras of the energy system. I have not found this to be the case in all people.

What I can feel is that there are four chakras located above the crown chakra and ascending higher. Below the root chakra, I have seen five chakras, one more than above the crown chakra. However, this has not always been the case and with some individuals, I will perceive more or less upper and lower chakras.

For simplicity sake, I call the ones below the root chakra "sub"-chakras and the ones above the crown chakra "supra"-chakras. So, there are generally five sub-chakras and four-supra chakras. And to reiterate, this is just my findings. I have had a difficult time finding sources that correspond with what I "see" and "feel".

With these sub and supra-chakras, I have found some connection between the two. When watching them open over time (and it does take time for these guys to open) it appears that first one will open and then the corresponding lower or upper chakra will open.

For example, let us say that we are looking at the chakra system of an individual whose seven main chakras are aligned, opened and balanced. We then look above their seven main chakras and see their first two "supra" chakras are also open while the remaining two supra-chakras are closed. To correspond with this, the individual's first sub-chakra will be open, and their second sub-chakra will be in a transitional state - working its way from closed to open. Their remaining three sub-chakras will be closed. Once this person's second sub-chakra opens fully, this will allow their third supra and sub-chakras to start to open as well.

So, in this way an individual can work to open up their supra and sub-chakras one level at a time slowly advancing up and ascending down. I know - a little confusing but isn't this world confusing as it is!

If you look for information on these chakras you will see that some individuals call the chakra above your crown chakra your Soul Star Chakra and the one below your root chakra your Earth Star Chakra. The lower chakras that I term sub-chakras are also called sub-personal chakras by some individuals. I think these names are pretty cool, so I use them occasionally, but they are an invention of the new age movement and with that their names are very "new-agey".

So, what do these chakras actually do? From my experience, these chakras are about experiencing a greater sense of connection to the divinity while also manifesting into existence your material desires. Those supra-chakras, those are your connection to "the other side", to the dimensions beyond this one, to the energy levels and vibrational frequencies that are difficult for our human bodies to perceive. Those sub-chakras, those are your access to manifesting your spiritual ideas into the earthly environment. Of taking your divinely inspired ideas and thoughts and creating a physical manifestation from them.

And, let us be honest, I have not found many individuals who have these chakras open and aligned. Only by peeking in (I know, totally not always considered ethical) on the chakras of some well-known psychics and mediums have I seen individuals whose supra and sub-chakras were opened or opening.

It feels like this is the realm of the healer, the psychic and the priest whose work opening up to the divine is at the forefront of their consciousness. The average joe on the streets may not ever experience what it is like to have all their transpersonal chakras opened and aligned, and that is a totally valid experience to have.

Chakra States

Now that we have made it through our discussion of the seven major chakras and the additional chakras you might be asking yourself- what does it mean to have an open chakra? A blocked chakra? An overactive chakra?

So below is my "cheat sheet" for what the energy looks like in different chakra states. This is just what I have found and how I read energy. Your path may lead you in a different direction - if it does, trust that and go with it.

Open Chakra

When a chakra is open energy is flowing through the chakra. Energy is coming in and leaving as it is needed. Pretty simple really! This is the open and balanced state that we aim for all our chakras to be in.

Closed Chakra

If a chakra is closed, you may be avoiding activities and thoughts associated with this chakra. Closed chakras are usually an indication that you have taken steps to stop this energy from entering your auric field. These steps could include a fear or a denial of the energy associated with this chakra. Emotional baggage and physical injuries or illness can also close a chakra.

Closed chakras occur to us all so they are not something to be scared of, just a little heads up of an area in your life or a section of your energy body that you need to pay a little more attention to.

Blocked Chakra

If a chakra is blocked, something is getting in the way of your chakra fully expressing itself. This could be the flow of energy to this chakra or it may be because of some negative thoughts or feelings. Blocked chakras are not a state in themselves. A chakra is either opened or closed, but the block is an additional state that occurs within either preexisting states.

If a chakra is open and blocked (while the root and crown chakras are open), I see that block as a tiny smudge on an otherwise open and healthy chakra. These smudges are sometimes caused by our allowing other individual's perceptions to influence us. Usually, this type of block is an outside force, something that is not internal, that is preventing your chakra from fully expressing. Injuries and illnesses can block chakras for a time, but so can ideas and thoughts from other individuals that we let into our energy field.

Think of it like this - say you are pretty decently self-confident. You generally believe you can do anything you want to do and have an opened and balanced solar plexus chakra. But then a co-worker says that you did a really shitty job on a project at work and you feel those words like a punch to the stomach. Ugh. This may end up creating a block on an otherwise healthy solar plexus chakra if you let your co-worker's words stick and affect you. The other scenario would be to let those words roll off you and accept that they are their opinion and do not have to be yours - then your solar plexus chakra would likely remain unblocked. See the difference?

There is one scenario that you may find all your chakras being blocked. This happens when either your crown and/or root chakra are closed. This is because a closed crown or root chakra cuts off one stream of energy and will lead to all your other chakras being blocked since they do not get their full power.

Our bodies have two main energy streams, one coming in from the top of our heads and one coming in from our root chakra and running along the length of our spinal column. If either of these chakras is closed to energy, then an entire stream of energy has difficulty entering our bodies and thus your remaining chakras will have blocked energy as well. I know - this kind of stinks. If just your root chakra is closed all the other open chakras will be blocked - it is no fun seeing what just one shut down chakra can do to your entire energy system.

Having a closed root or crown chakra is essentially like operating at half power. And guess what - a large chunk of our society is operating just like that. I have seen root chakras close very easily on people who do not get enough sleep or who spend too much time binge watching shows. I may have seen this first hand after a few days of watching every episode of a show on Netflix. That root chakra just closes right up, and all those chakras end up blocked.

Recently, I have seen chakras start to block for no apparent reason at all. This occurs when the energy in the environment is changing and transforming.

Warning, we are about to get pretty woo-woo here! Sometimes there are shifts in the energy of our dimension. You can track these major energy shifts through the planets. Think back to all the hoopla that occurred around the winter solstice of 2012 and all the doomsday predictions that existed. It was not world-ending kind of change that actually happened but instead an energy shift that occurred. When this kind of energy change happens those who are intuitive or clairvoyant may see many individuals chakras start to be blocked leading up to the event. I see this as our energy bodies getting ready to accept a new kind of energy.

Overactive Chakra

Along with all the worry of having a chakra that is closed or blocked and not functioning up to its potential, there are also times when a chakra is taking on too much energy. At these times the chakra is said to be open and overactive. This occurs when too much attention is being directed to one area of your life, usually at the expense of other areas. Having an overactive chakra for too long a period of time may result in a physical manifestation of this excess energy, meaning you could possibly get sick or your physical body may start to mirror the appearance of your energy body.

I see the most overactive chakras in the solar plexus area. This is particularly true for individuals with large egos - and in these instances, those physical attributes may start to creep in and you will see their bellies start to expand to compensate for the size of their larger solar plexus. This isn't the case with everyone with an overactive chakra, just a general trend that I have seen occur.

Transitional State

A chakra in a transitional state is in the process of changing - going from closed to open or open to closed. During this time, it vacillates between the two states as the process of opening or closing continues. When a chakra is in this state you may feel that this center of your body is functioning wonderfully at some moments and at other moments you may have doubt and uncertainty creep in.

This transitional state usually occurs because, in my view, chakras take time to open and close. Yes, there are moments when a chakra can all of a sudden close on you. But opening it back up may take a few days to happen. Usually, it is not as symbol a process as visualizing an open root chakra to have a chakra that has been closed for five years open back up. Again, just my opinion here from my experiences. If a chakra has been stuck in one position for a long period of time, it will take time for the energy body to get used to having it open again. During this time period, the chakra will be in a transitional state, getting used to the new energy experience.

Common Energy States

I have seen a lot of people freak out when I tell them that they have closed chakras. But, to be honest, 97% of the individuals who come to me for chakra readings have at least one closed chakras. This is not something abnormal, it is just the world we live in.

It is a difficult task to keep all your chakras open and functioning properly at all times. Even I, your great metaphysical guru, have closed chakras from time to time. It is perfectly normal. Just take a closed chakra as an indication of what area of your life you need to focus on and work to balance.

I will say, however, that those who do true energy work, be it healing or psychic channeling, tend to have opened and balanced chakras. If I read for someone and see that all their chakras are opened, the majority of the time (heck, all of the time - meaning every-single-time) this individual will practice some type of energy work on a daily basis.

Why is this? When people channel energy, even for other people, they get used to having their energy centers open and this becomes their natural state. Doing work for others, in turn, benefits the individual as well as the recipient.

This does not mean you need to go out and start practicing energy work for hire. Actually, just the opposite. Instead, once your energy body starts to regularly exist in this open state, then you may feel drawn to energy work.

Please, do not feel bad if your chakras are closed. What is the purpose of life if not to work on bettering ourselves?

Aura Basics

What is an aura?

Most of us have heard about our aura at one time or another. Some people may have even had a picture of their aura taken at new age shop or fair. But what exactly is an aura and what do the colors in your aura mean?

Everything has an aura, be it an animate or inanimate object. We generally talk about the auras of living things because they have more energy or juice running through them and thus are easier to see and feel. But all the objects around you are emanating their own aura or frequency, you just might not be aware of it.

Auras are simply electromagnetic energy. Being that they are energy, scientists can actually identify them, although there is no consensus in the scientific community as to the purpose of an aura.

In the human energy field, there are several layers that make up our auras. The easiest one to see is that of our etheric aura which extends just about an inch to two inches away from our body. This is a part of our aura that does not have a distinct color pattern.

Next is our astral aura. This is the part of our aura where bands of colors can be seen. Those closest to the etheric aura relate to our personality and may change very slowly over time based on our focus and interests, but generally stay consistent.

Farther away from these color bands will be colors and vibrations that denote what emotions we are currently feeling and those thoughts that are in our minds at the present time. Finally, the aura is all contained in an auric shell which looks like an egg shape around our bodies.

Some individuals will give more names and meanings to each of the layers of the aura - correlating them with the chakra system or giving them each their own category. This can be true, but I have found that, at least in the beginning, it is easier to lump the layers together.

Our auras are continuously active. They expand and contract depending on our environment and how we are emotionally feeling. If we are scared, feeling shy or threatened our auras will close in around us and visibly become smaller. When we are feeling relaxed and comfortable our auras expand outward and grow bigger. Generally, in a healthy individual, auras will extend about four or five feet outside their physical body.

Auras also contain information embedded in them. There may be holes or tears showing trauma that has occurred to the individual's physical or energetic body. Some, well really a great deal, of people have blocks in their aura which are an accumulation of energetic debris from situations that have not been properly dealt with.

All of this information is neat and interesting, but what most people want to know is what color their aura is and what does it mean...

Aura Colors

As you will hear me repeat throughout this book, everyone has different associations with certain things and you should follow what feels "right" for you. I have included in this book information on how I read and see colors so that it can act as a starting point for you. If you do not feel these color descriptions fit what you see then go with your way, not mine. My "blue" may be different than your blue and that is perfectly coolio with me!

Red

Individuals with auras that are red are physically motivated. These people generally have a lot of energy and may spend their free time engaged in athletic pursuits. These are the people that have a hard time sitting still and watching Netflix for hours a day and need to get up and *do* something. Red can also be found in individuals who have lots of anger or rage. Usually I don't see the red in an aura surrounding a person as representative of anger, but instead little spurts of energy may float out that represent anger. These energy "spurts" may stay in an aura for a period of time, but do not usually wrap around an aura unless the person is a completely angry person.

The most "red" representative I know is my father-in-law. He is the definition of a red aura. He has two speeds - either he is going around doing things or he is sitting on the couch sleeping. Not much lazy downtown. It is a little joke in our family that we regularly have to take him out on his "walk" - when everyone else is relaxing he will want to go on a two-mile hike. This is also an individual that, in his mid-60s, regularly rides his bike, attends spin class, hikes mountains and plays pickleball. Basically - a physically motivated individual.

Another example of individuals with red auras is young children. You will often see busy toddlers and preschoolers with a lot of red in their auras. This is a time in their lives that they are learning and experiencing with their bodies. Using their body each day is their main way of exploring and learning in their environment. This is why playgrounds are so popular with young children, but you don't see many adult playgrounds around.

Red is actually the first aura color that I randomly saw without even trying. This happened while I was sitting and eating lunch with my daughter who was at the time a toddler. I glanced over and noticed some red in her aura around her head and thought - hey, look at that!

Orange

Individuals with orange auras tend to be the creative and artistic types. They will find joy in the art of making. For example, artists, chefs, and musicians normally have a lot of orange in their auras. This color may come into an individual's aura when they are pursuing a creative activity like writing a book or choreographing a dance.

I also usually see this color in individuals who are pregnant, particularly around their belly if not throughout their entire aura. Pregnancy is a creative process in itself, so it is not surprising that this is the case.

My mother has a lot of orange in her aura, although other colors sometimes blot out the strength and persistence of this color. Throughout her life she has always had an interest in art, and, although she did not pursue art as a career, it has always been in the background. It has been interesting to watch the amount of orange shrink and grow over the years. Once she retired from a busy legal career, she was able to refocus on painting and the orange in her aura started to grow until it eventually extended throughout her auric field.

Yellow

Yellow is the most common color I see in individual's auras. This is the color of the person who thinks with their mind and not their heart. This is the color of the intellectual and business person. I see a lot of yellow around people that are in the process of gaining information, like students and teachers. I also see yellow as a representative of how our current culture operates and I believe this is why this color predominates most individual's auras.

I would say 70% of people I see have yellow somewhere in their auras. This color just means that the individual trusts more their rational mind as opposed to their feelings or their intuition. There is nothing bad about this, it is just how our society and culture currently vibe.

This is another color that I see prominently in children. As a society, we have children spend the majority of their days concerned with learning rational information. All that time spent in school lends most children to having yellow in their aura. Now if we retrained our focus to having our youth engage in more spiritual or intuitional pursuits, this likely would not be the case.

Green

Individuals with green in their auras tend to be healers. These people care deeply for others and are here to help in any way possible. Generally, doctors, counselors and social workers have green in their auras. When I see this color around an individual I know that they are likely helping someone in some capacity.

Different shades of green can also be associated with envy or jealous but, as with red and rage, these green pieces do not usually encircle an individual's entire energy. Instead, the green in an aura associated with jealousy will take up small sections or areas of the aura, particularly when they are expressing that emotion in the moment.

The same is true with green representing a spot of healing an individual is currently going through. I usually do not see green in this manner, but I know other individuals and clairvoyants see green relating to an individual going through healing, so I wanted to mention it here.

Remember too, that green in an aura doesn't necessarily have to mean an individual is a traditional healer. Energy healers usually have a strong green color in their aura as well. Those people who are just good listeners and like to help others solve problems may have green auras too.

The brightest green aura I have seen are usually those of doctors who spend most of their days focused on healing patients. I come from a family filled with doctors and those that really care for and are concerned with their patients will have deeper and more prominent green in their aura. My husband is one of those individuals, who generally cares about his patients and wants the best for them. Green is his main aura color and can be found throughout his auric field.

Pink

Individuals with pink auras are very caring and loving. This type of person will give of themselves and their time unconditionally. These individuals are highly altruistic, and you will likely see individuals with pink in their aura volunteering in their spare time or finding ways to help those in need. People with pink in their aura are usually very good friends and will likely remember birthdays and anniversaries.

If you encounter an individual with a lot of pink in their aura you will feel a sense of peace and calm. You may be drawn to the calm and serene sense of these individuals and just generally enjoy being around them. Sometimes when I am around someone that has a pink aura it just feels like the energy is a nice gentle hug.

One of my friends is the perfect representation of someone with a pink aura. I am lucky that we have been buddies since we were still in diapers. This is someone who gives the best hugs I have ever experienced, you know the strong and long hug that tells you she really loves and is concerned for you. She is also the friend that always remembers your birthday and sends a card in advance, so it gets to you before your actual birthday (I am horrible at doing this!). This is also someone who, after giving birth to her son, went back to preparing food for the local Meals on Wheels program before she even was ready to go back to work - I mean, what kind of person does that??? An individual with a bright pink aura!

Blue

I do not see a lot of individuals with blue in their aura. This is the color of someone involved in highly spiritual pursuits. Individuals with blue in their aura tend to be priests, counselors or authors. They may have a difficult time focusing on this plane of existence as their minds are normally wondering to bigger questions - like, what is the meaning of life and why are we here?

Those with blue in their aura will usually feel drawn to spirituality and religion, no matter what form it takes. These people will find their way to churches or places of worship and enjoy spending time in them.

This is a color I am particularly interested in as this is the main color in my aura. Throughout all my work reading auras I have only seen blue in a handful of people. Spirituality and religion are just not that prominent in the minds and lives of individuals in our society today.

As someone with blue as the most prominent color in my aura, I have been interested in religion and spirituality since I was a young child. I would regularly ask my parents to take me to church on Sunday (although they preferred to sleep in). I have always been drawn to spirituality and the occult - the type of religion and spiritual practice were not as important as the message. As an adult, I regularly attend church (although a highly metaphysical branch), read spiritual and philosophical books, and am a practicing witch. I've noticed that one of the three main ministers at our church has blue in their aura as well. So blue usually will signal someone whose spirituality is important, not just one day of the week but every day.

Indigo

Individuals with indigo in their auras are usually highly intuitive. They may have advanced clairvoyant abilities or experience vivid dreams. Usually, this color will start forming around an individual's head when they are beginning to open up their intuitive abilities and as they progress the color will extend down around to eventually encompass their entire aura.

This is a very interesting process to watch and I've been fortunate enough to have a few regular clients who have ordered readings every couple of months that allowed me to see this process take place. First, the indigo will only be found around the head area, but as they became more and more involved in the intuitive realm this color spread throughout their aura.

This color can also be found in individuals who use their intuitive abilities but would not admit to calling it that. Think about police officers who follow their "instincts" or doctors who just "know" what is the right treatment each time. I will normally see indigo in certain portions of the aura in these types of individuals. It usually does not extend fully until the individual takes further steps to develop and trust their intuition. But be certain that the best cops and doctors out there have indigo somewhere in their aura!

Purple

Individuals with purple auras are very spiritual but in a way of service to others as compared with blue individuals who are more concerned with their own personal spirituality. They are connected to a higher purpose and a higher calling. They may also have a strong connection to "higher source". Like individuals with blue in their aura, those with purple generally tend to be priests and counselors.

Purple is also considered a color of royalty and those that feel confident and in charge of their spirituality and lives may have this color in their aura. Think about those individuals that are seen as the top of their fields and strive to do good for those that follow their work. These types of individuals have a lot of purple in their aura.

Purple is another one of those colors that I do not see very often in my daily work. The main times I see this color is when "looking" at individuals such as James Van Praagh or Oprah who have a lot of purple in their auras (and yes, sometimes you can see auras through the tv screen!). And, surprisingly, my dog also has purple around his head in his aura. I believe this is because he is working on teaching some advanced spiritual lessons at this time in his life.

Brown

Brown in an individual's aura can mean several things. If someone is deeply connected with the earth, plant and animal life they may have a lot of brown show up in their aura. These individuals likely spend a lot of time with the soil and in their gardens.

Brown can also appear more as a muddied yellow and be associated with chronic mental or emotional issues. I see this brown form when individuals are spending too much time in their heads or too much time helping others and not practicing their own self-care.

In actuality, I see the brown associated with emotional issues much more often than that associated with people with strong connections to the earth. This color is common in mothers of young children who spend most of their time concerned with taking care of others instead of themselves.

In my personal life, I am around a large number of mothers and have noticed that brown and pink sometimes go hand in hand. A mother will have deep emotional and loving connections to their family members, but if they don't take enough time for themselves they also develop some resentment which leads to brown in the aura.

Grey

Grey in an aura can be tricky to read as, for me, it signals a time of transition. When grey encompasses the entirety of an aura sometimes this will mean that the individual is adding a color to their vibrational frequency and if I check back in a day or two I will see the grey is gone and, in its place, a new color will appear. But grey can also signal a location that is starting to or susceptible to physical pain - one that may eventually shift to black.

I also see grey show up in women who are either currently menstruating or going through menopause. If this is the case the grey will appear over their pelvic region and, if they are menstruating, will go away in a day or two. And in case you are wondering, yes, it is weird to be able to tell a client that I know it is their time of the month!

People who suffer from chronic pain or depression will also have a lot of grey in their aura. My mother is one of those individuals who seems to always be in pain. She has multiple degenerative disks throughout her spine as well as a foot that is numb and generally in pain. Let's just say that she usually has grey in large portions of her aura. Her degenerative disks are hereditary, so I have been taking steps to prepare my body for this possibility by doing yoga regularly and keeping healthy. I know that when I see so much grey in her aura that she is in pain and I do not look forward to the same thing happening in my aura.

Black

Individuals with black spots or holes in their aura may be undergoing physical trauma or pain. This color is normally delegated to just the location of the pain and can be used to pinpoint the source of a physical problem. I usually only see black located in designated areas, but occasionally I have seen black located throughout a person's aura when that individual has constant chronic pain (aka my mother).

When some people see an aura that is filled with black they wonder if that individual is about to die. Don't worry, that is not usually the case. The aura instead turns a white color when a person is about to make a transition.

I have also heard, but not actually seen, that black can be found in an aura of someone who is truly evil. I would imagine that this would be the most prominent color in the aura, but, like I said, I have been fortunate enough not to have ever seen this in person or from my clients.

Gold

So, I used to say that gold and silver were rare colors to have in an individual's aura but I don't believe that anymore as I have seen them in many people's auras.

When gold is located throughout a person's aura it usually means that this person is a medium or has some form of communication with individuals who used to be living and now have crossed over - aka this person likely has a talent for talking to the dead.

I will caution you, however, that this does not mean that the individual knows they can do this or has this skill, just that they could if they developed it. I say this because gold is one of the (many) colors that are in my aura, but I do not go around telling people that their dead grandmother is standing right behind them. I may later develop this ability, but right now it is not something that I focus on.

But, I will say that I have seen this color in every medium that I know. All those mediums with shows on tv have gold throughout their auric field. This is a signal to me on whether someone is a true medium or just faking it.

I also see the color gold when someone has a loved one that is visiting them and enters their auric field. Usually, when this happens I see this as a spot of gold over the right shoulder in a person's aura, not as gold covering or close to their physical body.

Silver

When I see silver in an individual's aura I know they have a strong connection to their spirit guides or celestial entities. This color is usually present in individuals with very strong and well-developed psychic and intuitive skills.

Silver is the color I see for spirit guides and those entities that have not lived a recent human existence and I will therefore sometimes see silver over shoulders of individuals when they are working directly with their guides, similar to gold in individuals with loved ones coming to visit.

In my experience, the color silver is almost like an advanced version of the color indigo. I have never seen silver in the aura of an individual who did not have indigo somewhere in their aura as well.

As mediums have their gold, I believe psychics have their silver. Those individuals who are adept at reading energy patterns and are true psychics usually have silver throughout their aura.

White

For me, white is the rarest color to see when reading an aura. It is the color that signals absolute divinity. The only form I have seen this color is in bits and specks in individuals who were in the process of healing. I have never seen white be a prominent color in anyone's aura or even take up large sections.

I have heard, but have not had the opportunity to see, that white occurs in an individual's aura as they transition to the other side. Bodies that are in this transitional state will have their aura's turn completely white just before the process begins.

Aura Conditions

In addition to your aura having different colors, there can also be different conditions or consistencies that your aura can take on. The most likely states are blocks, holes or tears. However, I have seen everything from auras looking like they had galaxies inside them to those that looked like marshmallows and electrical storms.

These auric conditions can have many different sources, from physical to emotional and energetic energy. Finding out the reason behind these disturbances in the aura can help you heal your energetic body. Healing the energetic body will sometimes also speed up any physical symptoms you may have as well.

Since the different states vary so greatly, I am only going to spend time on the most prominent ones here. But if you develop a keen eye for seeing auras be aware that other states exist. Use your intuition and psychic abilities to discover the "why" behind these states and figure out how to heal them.

Blocks

Individuals can have blocks form in their aura when they are "blocking" or denying something about themselves. Blocks sometimes develop through strong emotional experiences as well, particularly those that you experience but then stop before all the emotions are released. For example, you may have gone through a death in your family but were unable to grieve fully. By stopping the grieving process, you may end up creating a block in your energetic aura.

Usually, these blocks will have a color associated with them such as black or grey. I have never seen a block in an individual's aura where the color of their aura didn't change as well in that location. This is why you can use color to help "see" where there is an issue in the aura, then dive deeper to really determine the cause of that color.

When focusing on blocks you can sometimes "feel" what is causing them. This could be something in the individual's current life or brought over from a past life. By reading these blocks you can find insight into the "why" behind certain physical issues in someone's life.

The most prominent block I have seen is in women who desperately want to get pregnant but are unable to. In these individuals, they will sometimes have a grey or black area that will develop in their aura around their pelvis. By "reading" these spots intuitively, I can then pinpoint the energetic "why" to why the individual is having a difficult time getting pregnant. I have seen everything from past life issues to anxiety preventing pregnancy. Sometimes all it takes is acknowledging the existence of this block to then allow it to fall away. This may take the form of finally finding out the physical reason for the lack of fertility or just priming the body to be ready to accept an embryo.

Holes

Holes can also develop in an individual's aura. These holes can be associated with a myriad of things including emotional or physical trauma.

With holes, there will not always be an associated color change in the aura. The color in the individual's aura may be intact with just a hole in a specific location unless the individual is exposing themselves to a negative environment or one that does not "vibe" with their energetic frequency. Then this hole can let in energy that is not common to the individual and the color in the aura may change.

The issue with holes is that they allow energy to enter an individual's auric field even if they don't want to accept that energy. Personally, I tend to get holes in my aura in front of my heart area and on the bottoms of my feet. There is no grey or black in this part of my aura for me. What this hole does is make it so that sometimes I feel too much and can take on the emotions of individuals very easily. This is common in empaths and makes it so usual techniques to push away energy for empaths do not always work. This is an area of my aura that I constantly work on, making sure the holes close up when I find them. Later I will give you my go-to source for sewing up these holes!

Tears

An aura develops tears when the physical body has trauma or surgery. I read a tear similar to a hole only its source is from the physical instead of the emotional or energetic body.

Going through a medical procedure you may find that your physical body is able to heal faster than your auric and energetic body. That wound may be sensitive energetically long after it has healed physically. With that in mind be sure to be careful with what energy you expose yourself to after having minor or major surgery.

So, what does this mean in practical terms? After having surgery, you should be cautious about going to large public places and venues with a lot of people. You should likely not spend the Saturday after surgery at the mall or sporting event. Instead, protect your energetic field and allow yourself time to heal on all fronts.

Energy Basics

Okay, now you have a basic overview of both the chakra system and auras. Yeah, you! Before we get to the fun part of learning how to actually tell how your chakras and aura are functioning, we have to learn a few more basics. No whining - I can hear you out there grumbling about the basics, but it is important to know the actual properties of energy. This will give you a good basis for paying attention to energy in general, which will then help your skill with understanding chakras and auras. Plus, you will likely realize that you have been sensing energy all along and just didn't realize it!

What Does Energy Feel like?

Energy is all around us. We are made of energy. That book next to your nightstand is made of energy - your car - your cat - that mean thought about your boss - even your mother-in-law is made of energy. But why do all these things look and feel so different?

It all has to do with the qualities that the energy has. And guess what - if you focus and pay attention, you can feel the energy around you that your eyes may not be able to see (although you can *see* energy too - more on that next).

What qualities will you be able to pick up on?

The thing is, in our modern culture we just do not take the time to pause and really observe what our environment is like around us. We have, to some effect, lost a great deal of the sensitivity that is inherent in us and which we are born with. How often do you just take a few breaths when you enter a new environment to *feel* what it is like? I'm guessing your answer is going to be not very often. We don't value our feelings because they are harder to quantify and objectify (but not impossible). Science is the predominant religion in our society and if we can't see it, it is hard for us to believe it.

But that has not always been the case and there are ways that you can rediscover your own sensitivity to energy. First, you need to understand the different qualities that energy possesses, and you may realize that you have been sensing energy all along - you just didn't know how to describe it.

One prominent distinction is the density of the energy around you. If you have ever been in a room where people are in contention and mad with each other, you may have just felt a heaviness around you. If there is a specific location that someone was standing in when they expressed intense negative emotions, you can run your hands through it and it may feel different from the other energy in the room. Think about the phrase "the tension in the room is so *thick* you could cut it with a knife" - there is some truth to this saying!

The opposite of heavy energy is a lighter feeling energy. You can probably guess what light energy usually signals

- feelings of love. Love is a high vibration feeling and with it comes a lightness.

Along with density, energy will also feel hot or cold. If you watch any ghost shows or read any books on the topic you might have heard that ghosts sometimes show up as cold spots. Ghosts, whatever your thoughts on them, are residual energy and thus they will have qualities of energy as well - which includes temperature. When you are in a conversation with someone that becomes "heated" see if you can feel that heat exchange between the two of you.

There are additional ways you may feel energy if you are aware and take the time to notice. Energy may feel "tingly" or like "pinpricks". You may also feel energy flowing or being stagnant. Just pay attention to your interactions with other people and see if you can discern a difference.

Exercises you can do to feel energy right away

Perhaps one of the most popular ways to grasp the concept of feeling energy is to sense it between your hands. To do this, first rub your hands together quickly to open up your hand chakras which will make feeling energy easier. Next slowly pull your hands apart about five inches and then slowly move them closer together a few inches. Does it feel like there is something *thick* and *heavy* between your hands? Repeat this a few times and see what qualities this energy has.

Now take that energy you are feeling and try rolling it into a ball like you would with play-dough. Take that ball of energy and move it to the back of one of your hands.

Does it feel different? Now switch hands and put the energy ball on the back of your other hand. Does this feel the same or different? Energy can sometimes feel different between your two hands. Now move this energy ball around your body, over your face, your legs, your toes. What areas of your body feel the most sensitive?

This subtle force you are feeling is energy. The more you practice this exercise and understand what energy actually is, the easier it will be for you to feel it when you are out and about.

What Does Energy Look like?

Now that we have discussed what energy *feels* like, let's take a look (get it, *look*, hehe) at what energy actually *looks* like. This section is my personal observations on energy and may not reflect what other clairvoyants or psychics view when looking at energy. But, as with anything, it is always helpful to know how other individuals perceive these subtle energies. Sometimes it only takes someone pointing it out to realize you have been seeing energy all along and just didn't realize it!

Waves

The most obvious way I see energy is in what looks like little waves coming off of an object. This is similar to what you can see coming from the asphalt on a hot summer day - those heat waves.

For me, I will see these waves as something akin to leftover energy that is stuck in a location. If someone has experienced intense emotions they may leave some energy in that area and then, later on, I may come along and bump into it. This happens frequently at the yoga studio I attend where people will release pent-up emotions while they are in a pose and then sometimes that energy lingers in that spot after they leave.

I have also seen these waves of energy around an animal that was about to cross-over. It felt like the soul or spirit of the cat I was looking at was already disassociating from her physical body and wasn't fully present. These waves appeared above and touching her physical body.

Static

Another form that energy takes for me is that of static. It looks almost like the static on a tv screen, only the little black spots are throughout the environment. This energy is everywhere I look, and I view it akin to the energy web on which this physical plane exists. In my everyday life, I just ignore it and it fades into the background, but if I choose to focus on it, it comes to my attention.

When I focus on this static web I will also hear the increase in pitch and sound in my ears that is accompanied by my connection to a higher source or my spirit guides. When I see this energy, I know that I am focusing on a more spiritual plane of existence and not the material plane we reside. It is in this space that I may also see the specks of light associated with my spirit guides or angels.

Tendrils

Sometimes energy also appears as tendrils floating around almost like clouds in the sky. For me, this energy usually takes on a blueish color and I see it most frequently on ceilings and in dark environments. To see these tendrils, I usually need to be in a completely calm and relaxed state and then these guys will appear, as opposed to the static that I can see even after having three cups of coffee.

I am not exactly sure what these tendrils of energy actually are, but I imagine them as messages and thoughts sent between sources. It feels like energy is moving from one location to another and these are the connecting lines between the two.

What Does Energy Sound like?

Yeah, you never thought about energy having a sound frequency, did you? The truth is, our human ears have a difficult time picking up on the variety and levels of frequency that energy emits.

One thing that many people have experienced and are a common sign of an increase in energy frequency is a ringing in the ears. When connecting with a higher source you may notice the sound in your ears start to get louder and higher.

You can also *hear* your guides who are energy. What is confusing is that most people think that when they are going to hear from their guides it will be a big noise outside their body shouting at them. Truth is, that does not normally happen. I have only had that sort of communication from my guides a handful of times, and usually only when I am in deep meditation or in that period between sleep and wakefulness.

Instead, the most common way you will hear your guides is through that small quiet voice in your head. This will sound a lot like yourself just thinking and it takes time to distinguish between your ego talk and your guides talk. One way to determine the difference is to concentrate on if this is information that you know or if it seems totally random.

Personally, I hear my guides sometimes say single words when I am checking in on the energy of the day or doing a client reading. I may get a clairvoyant image appear in my third eye and then a word or phrase to go along with it.

Before I had developed my psychic abilities to the level they were at, my guides were still able to communicate with me this way, but I never really realized it. They did this most often in the form of songs that would suddenly appear in my mind as if out of nowhere. The most prominent memory of this is on the morning of my scheduled C-section. I woke up with the song "Quiet Waters" playing gently in my mind and I knew that my guides were right there beside me.

Discovering your Energetic Body

Now I dub you - one with basic knowledge of the energetic body. Do you feel like you have been seeing and feeling energy all your life and you just weren't aware of it? We are all psychic and sensitive, but it takes focus to settle ourselves down and really concentrate on what we are perceiving to realize that this energy is not *that* difficult to recognize.

Now we are going to start the fun part - the reason you likely picked up this book in the first place - how to see your aura and know the state of your chakras. We will start by working our way through our senses to understand how each sense can help us determine the state of our energy system.

First, we will look at sight, both with our eyes and our third eye, and determine how we can *see* our aura and chakras. Next, we will look at touch and understand how to tell the status of our energy through feeling our chakras and aura. We will continue on with the sense of sound and see how to hear the states of your energetic system. Following this we will look at just knowing, how can we quickly examine our life and just know and understand the color of our aura and the state of our chakras. Finally, we will wrap up with a good way to double-check your findings and determine if you are seeing, feeling, hearing and knowing your energy correctly.

And you may have noticed that I did not include taste. If you can tell me someone's aura colors by using the sense of taste I will be truly amazed! Now that would be something interesting to see! But since I have never witnessed it or known of its existence, we are skipping that great sense of taste in this exploration.

I also want to mention here, as a caution, I am going to teach you how to determine the energy in *your* body. If you want to look and feel the energetic body of someone else I strongly recommend performing some basic energy protection. It is all too easy to go about feeling someone's aura and then having their energetic problems stick to you or be absorbed by you if you are not practicing energetic protection. I know, when you tell your sister about this awesome book you are reading she is going to want you to "read her". Just be cautious. Fair warning here.

How to See your Chakras and Aura

I've got a secret to tell you...not all people who "see" energy see it with their physical eyes. I know - totally not what you have learned from television and movies! Not all people literally "see dead people" and not all people see energy. Instead, another method of "seeing" energy is to actually use your third eye and view it from that inner place. I know - not what you were thinking.

But before we get to seeing with that extra eye, we are going to focus on using your actual eyes, because this is likely what you imagine when you hear about people looking at auras.

Seeing auras with your physical eyes

I have never been able to see chakras with my physical eyes (only that extra third eye) and I don't know anyone who can do this, so for this section on seeing energy in the literal sense, I am going to stick with what I know - auras. With auras, the act of seeing the colors and being able to differentiate between them is accomplished by training and strengthening your physical eye muscles. You must learn to use your eyes in a manner that focuses on these colors and energy that is not apparent from your everyday reality.

How do you do this? There are some decent pictures and charts available out there that you can look at on a daily basis that will help strengthen your eye muscles. The late great metaphysician Ted Andrews wrote a book called How to see Auras and, in this book, he describes some wonderful exercises you can use to strengthen your eye muscles which will allow you to perceive auras. He explains in detail how to create these images for yourself and how to use them. I also really like the work of Sandy Anastasi who includes an image on the front of her Psychic Development series of books which will help those eye muscles. And you can always pick up one of those Magic Eye books that were popular in the 90's.

But, of course, my favorite resources are free resources. Did you know that the makers of Magic Eye have pictures available online that you can look at and practice with? You can also find other individual's pictures by searching online. One thing that needs to be clear though is that it takes time and patience to strengthen your eye muscles. This is not something that is going to happen overnight -

I mean, it could, but again I've never heard of this happening!

What you can start to see right away is the subtle energy body that exists within an inch or two of your skin. Some people see this energy as yellowish color while for others it takes on a bluish-green hue.

As with anything, there are a lot of different methods for learning to see this as well. Many people recommend staring at yourself in the mirror, concentrating on the spot in the middle of your forehead and then through your periphery you will be able to start to see your aura. I've always found this technique difficult because it requires you to A) have a neutral color background behind your mirror and B) stand there staring at yourself in the mirror. Try this too often and the people you live with will start to think you are a bit conceded!

The method I prefer is to take a blank piece of white paper and put your hand on top of it. Now play with the focus of your vision. Let your attention go to that place between your eyebrows and up a little - your third eye - and use your physical eyes to look at your hand. Now relax your eyes but don't let them loose total focus - difficult right! Play around with it and try it when you have a few minutes. See if you can see anything.

Once you get your eye muscles strong enough to see auras you likely won't go about your daily life seeing the aura of everyone you encounter. You will have to take the time and patience to focus and *want* to see the aura. Although, there are occasions when you may find yourself seeing auras when you don't plan to. This happened to me one day while at my daughter's dance class. The mothers were all sitting around drinking their coffee while our kids danced in the other room.

Suddenly, I noticed that the woman sitting just feet from me had red in her aura around her head and yellow around the rest of her body. I was not planning or trying to determine the color of her aura, it just happened. In reality, the reason I think this occurred was that I had done a reading for a client before the class and was sipping on my third cup of coffee. For me, this combination tends to "open things up" and that left me seeing a clear aura when I didn't mean to. Just imagine trying to carry on a conversation while pretending you aren't noticing someone's aura!

But I want to be honest, this is not the goal of these exercises. The goal is not to be able to randomly see the other dance mom's aura. Instead, what this tells me is that I did not properly ground my energy after the reading I did and had too much of it flowing through me. What it told me was that I needed to take some breaths and let that extra energy be released back into the ground.

And the final caveat I want to provide about seeing the actual colors in auras is that not everyone will be able to accomplish this. I find many people get frustrated and tired of the constant practice it takes to get to this point. It is not something you can rush. This is a skill that for many people, myself included, takes years (not months - years) to develop and hone.

Seeing auras and chakras with your third eye

Now if you want to see your aura and your chakras with your third eye, you are also going to need to practice strengthening a different muscle - the third eye muscle. Any activity that strengthens your third eye in general will work, but it is also helpful to focus on exercises that work primarily with the energetic body.

To do this look at a full-length photo of yourself or stand in a mirror where you can see the full view of your body. Move your inner awareness, that inner sense of you, up to that third eye area. Take a few deep breaths and relax - there is no test, so you don't need to get anything right.

With your awareness at that third eye area *look* and see what colors encompass your body. Remember, you aren't actually seeing the colors with your eyes, they will just be on the image of you in your mind. And sometimes, you won't even see the color surround you instead you will just see a brief flash of the color in your mind. This is all legit and you should take note of it.

Some people prefer to do this exercise with their eyes closed. If this is the case for you, simply see an image of yourself in your mind's eye and ask yourself what colors are in your aura. Pay attention to any images you receive.

Now scan your body up and down over the areas where your chakras are. Do you sense any energy? Is there a lot? A little? Does the energy look open or closed? What do the colors in your chakras *look* like? Are they bright and shiny? Are they muddy? Notice anything that comes to your mind and acknowledge it.

Try this exercise a few times a week and see if you pick up on the same color(s) of your aura each time or the same chakra balance. Is there one color you perceive the most? This is likely your dominant aura color. A chakra that always seems brown instead of a bright color? Remember, sometimes it takes time to acknowledge your logical mind and let it calm down before you can let this sight come through.

As your psychic senses strengthen and develop *seeing* auras and chakras will become easier and easier. This skill takes time so do not give up if you don't get it the first time around.

How to Feel your Chakras and Aura

Feeling your chakras and auras can be a good way to start opening up to the energetic body and learning more about it. If you tried the exercise in the section on "what energy feels like" then, guess what, you have already felt your aura! Pretty cool right!

Feeling the Aura

If you want to continue practicing feeling your aura, you can do so by moving your hands about an inch or two over your entire body. Sense when the energy feels denser or cooler or any difference you can discern. Note down anything you feel and repeat this exercise every couple of days. Sense if there is a pattern forming. Do you always feel a heat coming from your right knee and this just happens to be a location that acts up each time you play tennis? Then maybe there is some stuck energy there.

If you are adept at this you may even learn how to feel the different colors of energy - although, I must admit I have never done this myself. Colors have different vibrations, so you can work on sensing each vibration with your hands. You can practice this by taking items of each color and place your hand over each to *feel* the difference. Any item will work for this exercise, but choosing things made out of the same substance but different colors may work best. This could require a trip to the craft store where you can purchase small pieces of felt of each color. Put your hand on each and see if you can sense the differences between the colors. Then put your hand over your aura and see if you can feel what color is most similar.

Don't feel discouraged if you can't feel energy this way. Each person has a different skill set that they are most adept at. Feeling colors is not something that is in my skill set, but I know that if I practiced it every day I would be able to add this to my tool bag.

Feel the Chakras

Feeling the energetic state of chakras may be a little easier than differentiating between the different colors of the aura. This is a technique I learned during Reiki training, but it can be useful in any situation.

Start out opening your hand chakras as you did when you felt your aura. Then take your hands and place them about five inches away from each chakra. Move your hands up and down sensing where the energy feels most dense and where you stop feeling it.

Go from one chakra to the next and see if you can *feel* a difference. Does the energy feel more prominent in one section of your body and almost nonexistent at another? Does one section feel warmer or cooler than another? Remember all the ways we can use to describe energy - how do you describe the energy at each chakra on your body?

As with all these exercises, repeating them over the span of days and weeks will help you become more efficient. Sense if your energy feels different from one day to the next. Maybe if you get into a heated argument see if you can excuse yourself to a private place and check your chakras - do they feel different? How about after watching a funny show on tv or a scary movie - anything change? Keep trying and practicing and your hand chakras will become more sensitive and attuned.

How to Hear your Chakras and Aura

Remember when we discussed what energy sounds like. Those subtle sounds inside your head. If you are primarily clairaudient you may find that you can actually hear the state of your chakras and aura.

How do you do this? Look at your root chakra or say the words root chakra in your head and listen if you hear any words. Does the word open come to you? How about closed? What about if the word "dog" comes to you. Acknowledge each word and write it down for later - no matter how silly it sounds.

After some time, you may find a pattern developing. Maybe, for you, the word dog means that your chakra is open because you constantly have to open the door to let your dog out. Don't discount funny or unusual words - they may end up having a meaning for you.

You can do this with your aura as well. Say your name in your head or just ask yourself what colors are in your aura. Do any words come to mind? Any colors? Again, don't discount unusual words. Maybe you hear the word broccoli and come to learn that broccoli means you have green in your aura.

Keep practicing this and see what you get. Being persistent and seeing patterns will help you discern what the meaning behind the words are. Of course, if you just hear colors and specific chakra states your life will be a lot easier!

How to Know about your Chakras and Aura

A super easy way anyone can figure out what their energy system is like is to just be aware of your everyday self and life. For your chakras, think about how you feel and what you spend your time doing. Do you feel a little flighty and spend 90% of your time on social media? Then it is pretty likely that your root chakra is closed. Have you recently gone through a hard breakup and have vowed never to love again, maybe that heart chakra needs some balancing? Look at your life and look at the information in the section about each chakra. Does it sound like that area of your life is balanced and functioning properly? And this is the total truth zone - you may have to get brutally honest with yourself here.

For your aura colors think about what colors you feel drawn to. What color has everyone just associated with you? For me, most of my friends would easily guess that my favorite color is blue, and this is the main color in my aura. As a kid my bedroom walls were painted blue, my carpet was blue and even my husband got me a blue diamond for my engagement ring. Yep, I'm pretty obvious.

Now think about yourself. What is your favorite color to wear? What was your favorite color when you were a kid? Look around your house, what colors dominate? One interesting correspondence I have found is that sometimes people's yoga mats will reflect their main aura colors. This isn't a set rule by it has been true about 70% of the time.

This is just a laid back and fun way to think about what your chakras and aura may look like. Like anything using your logical mind and not your intuition, this isn't going to be correct all the time, but it can give you a starting point.

The Pendulum Method

My favorite and the easiest way for newbies to learn to see and differentiate the different colors in your aura and determine the state of your chakras is to use a pendulum. This method is also good to use to help you confirm whether what you get using the other methods is correct. There is a reason I left this method for the end - you will soon learn that it may become all too easy to rely on this technique.

Pendulum Basics

A pendulum is basically an object attached to a string. Some people use rings or buttons connected to a string as their pendulum while others purchase pendulums made of woods or crystals from stores. Personally, I found that, for this type of work, a pendulum made out of crystal works best. This also is very dependent on your personal vibrations and energy level. Try out a variety of pendulums and see which one resonates and works for you best.

How do you know if a pendulum works for you? Take it and hold it at one end and then ask it which direction is "yes". Then ask it which direction is "no". If it moves and responds easily than it will work!

Growing up I had a beautiful pendulum made out of some type of metal, maybe brass. This pendulum worked great for finding the lost tv remote and other mundane activities. But as I grew older and increased my vibration, that metal pendulum no longer resonated with me. I could not get it to react to the energy of chakras - it would just sit there not moving. I had to go to a metaphysical store and try out their crystal pendulums to get something that would work with my higher vibrational frequency. I currently use a clear quartz pendulum for the majority of my work. Try out a variety and see what works best for you.

Using the Pendulum to Determine Aura Colors

Now that you have your pendulum it is time to get it working for you! First, we will examine how to tell what color is in your aura.

For this exercise, take a blank sheet of paper and write out all the different colors of the aura on it. There is no particular method to this, write them however you see fit. If you are creative and have the tools on hand you can even draw little circles with the different aura colors in them all over the piece of paper.

Personally, I like to leave a blank spot in the middle of my piece of paper as a central location for your pendulum to start and then I write out all the colors around this spot. You can be as creative as you want with this step - it is all up to you.

Next, you want to form some connection between the piece of paper with the aura colors on it and the person's aura you are reading. If you are reading your own aura simply touch the paper with one hand to establish this connection. Alternately, you can also write your name on that center blank location where the pendulum rests.

Now, holding your pendulum in your other hand about three inches above the piece of paper, ask your higher self to tell you what color(s) are in your aura. The pendulum should move and swing to one color. Note what color it is pointing to by saying, either mentally or out loud, the color. If this is correct the pendulum should then swing in the "yes" direction before moving onto the next color if there is one. Repeat this process. For me, when the pendulum has told me all the colors in an individual's aura it will then go back to the first color it mentioned.

For example, if I was reading my own aura I would touch the piece of paper with my left hand to establish a connection. Then holding the pendulum in my right hand over the piece of paper I would ask what colors are in my aura (you don't have to do this out loud - it can be silently as well). Then I would watch the pendulum move as it swung toward the main color in my aura. I silently acknowledge that color by saying the name - "blue" - then it swings in the clockwise direction for "yes" before moving to the next color. This process continues until all the colors of my aura have been mentioned and then the pendulum will swing back to blue again.

After you have a list of colors in your aura you can then work on figuring out where these colors are located. For this, take either a full-length picture of yourself or you can draw a picture on another sheet of white paper. I am not great at drawing pictures of people, so for me, this takes the form of a stick figure drawn on a white piece of paper. Yep - I work pretty basically here, you do not have to get fancy if you don't want to!

Now again establish that connection with this new sheet of paper by touching it with one hand while holding your pendulum with the other hand over the figure. Look at your list of colors in your aura and ask, "where in my aura is the color _____?".

Position your pendulum at the head of your picture and note what direction the pendulum is swinging. Is it swinging "yes" or "no"? Move your pendulum over the picture and discern where in the image the pendulum swings yes to and where it says no. This is the location of this color in your aura.

If the pendulum swings yes over the whole body, then this color likely covers your complete aura. Also, note to what extent the pendulum is swinging - does it swing in large circles or small? Large circles tend to mean that the color is stronger in your aura. I have found that usually, the order that I receive the colors in the beginning stages corresponds to the strength and amount of body that the color covers. Repeat these steps for all the colors in your aura.

If you find a color that you received was in your aura, but you can't find the location, try checking out the back of your picture. Turn the picture over and move the pendulum over it - does it say "yes" now? Alternatively, you can also double check the color by itself to make sure you got it right the first time.

Using the Pendulum to Determine Chakra States

Now that we know the colors in your aura, let's use this technique to find out if your chakras are opened or closed.

For this, you can again use the same full-length photo of yourself. If you do not have this, take a blank piece of paper and write out the chakras in order moving from the top to the bottom. If you have them available, you can also use various representations of the chakras such as a stone or card that represents the chakra instead or in addition to the picture/paper method.

Now that you have your representation of the chakras available, form that connection - touch the paper or place your hand near the stones. Take your pendulum and move it over each chakra noting the direction the pendulum is swinging.

For me, my pendulum moves clockwise for an open chakra, counter-clockwise for a closed chakra and back and forth for a blocked chakra. If a chakra is in a transitional state the pendulum will move first one direction then the next, such as counter-clockwise then clockwise. The first direct that pendulum moves is the original state of the chakra and the next direction is the state the chakra is moving towards. Also, remember that a chakra can be opened and still blocked so I always wait for a pause after the pendulum swings to the open position before moving on to the next chakra to see if the pendulum will additionally swing back and forth. Repeat this process for each chakra.

For example, let us say I have a full-length photo of myself and I want to know the state of my chakras. I will touch this photo with my left hand while raising the pendulum, with my right hand, over the area of my head on the picture. During this exercise, the pendulum moves to the clockwise position, so I know this chakra is open. Still, I wait a few seconds and watch. The pendulum then starts to move back and forth signaling that this chakra is also blocked. I will then move on to the next chakra, the third eye chakra, and repeat this process. Knowing myself and my chakras I would know that if my third eye chakra is also opened I should still wait because it would likely be blocked as well. For me, the natural state of my upper chakras is open and when they are also blocked it usually means that my root chakra is closed. If you remember from information on chakra states, if either the root or crown chakra are closed the rest of the chakras will be blocked even if they are opened.

Okay - now you have all the tools you need to examine the state of your chakras and the color of your aura! Congratulations, you now have the power to know when your energetic body is healthy and when it needs some work. Try out each method and see what works best for you. You can also combine the methods and find something that resonates with your strengths.

Balance your Energetic Body

Now that you know about your chakras and aura and how to find out what state they are in, you may be wondering what to do next. It is great knowing that your solar plexus chakra is blocked but how do you fix it? Well, this chapter will teach you a variety of methods that you can use to fix these energetic imbalances.

There is also a reason that I have included both the chakra system and auras into the same book. I often find that when a chakra is out of balance there will be some energy blockage showing up in the aura around that location as well. By balancing your chakras, you may find that those black, grey and brown spots in your aura clear up without any other specific methods.

And, because we live in a litigious society, I am going to reiterate that nothing I say here is to be used as medical advice. I am a psychic, not a doctor. I do believe in the power of western medicine, especially when it is combined with energy work.

So, talk to your doctor about any physical problems you may have. I am here to help with the energetic body. By balancing the energetic body, you can, in turn, help the physical body.

The Power of Thought

Thoughts have power. Most religious texts state this. Most metaphysical writers harp on this. There is even some science that proves the power of thought. So why do we go about our day with our thoughts in the gutter?

By paying close attention to what you are thinking and where your mind wonders, you can help control and bring back into balance your chakras and aura. Sounds like a mighty task though right! I mean, how are we supposed to pay attention to our thoughts 24 hours a day! I can meditate for about an hour tops but after that, my mind starts to wonder.

Well, fear not my friend! I have some practical tips for you to use to help with those pesky thought patterns. I am always a fan of good practical advice you can put into practice right away!

The Media You Consume

The first thing I recommend, and probably the hardest, is to pay attention to what you watch, read, hear, listen to, consume. The media we are exposed to on a daily basis has a large effect on our thought patterns. Don't believe me - just watch a scary movie and see how well you sleep tonight. Now think about all the things you just casually expose yourself to throughout the day. Did you see an image of a dead person on tv today, real or fictional? Were there instances of fear or violence in that book you are reading? Heck, did you turn on the news for at least five minutes today?

Any of these activities can affect our thoughts and where your mind goes throughout the day. You are what you eat - you are what you watch. So, if your thoughts have the power to help balance and cleanse your energetic body why not put them in their proper place.

Try it. Turn off the news. Limit your time on social media - yes, try to only check Facebook once or twice a day - I know, pretty difficult! Pay attention to what you have lined up in your Netflix queue - is it wholesome television or is it violent?

How about this - just try it for one week. Spend one week limiting the amount of violence and fear you expose yourself to. How do you feel at the end of the week? Does your life seem a little brighter? Does your energy feel balanced and aligned?

Words, Affirmations, and Mottos

Along with what media you consume look at what words are around you. Words themselves have a vibrational energy and these vibrations have been proven to affect the very essence and makeup of water. And guess what - you are made up of a lot of water! Just look at the research of Dr. Emoto.

So, what should you do about this? How about surrounding yourself with positive words and affirmations. Just like watching positive shows on tv, you can expose yourself purposely to positive words.

I decided one day that the shirts that I wear should have a positive message on it. Take this one step further, I wanted each shirt to have the word love on it. Love has a very high vibration. By wearing these shirts, I would help to raise my vibration by seeing the word every time I got dressed or looked in the mirror. Additionally, my theory is that when I interacted with people throughout my day they would also read the word love on my shirt and their vibrational frequency would then increase.

I have slowly built up a small collection of shirts that fit these criteria and continue to buy them up whenever I see them available. It is my small way of helping my energetic body as well as other individuals by a simple task of being mindful of what I wear.

Another way you can put this into practice is through the use of positive affirmations or mottos. I know, these get a bad rap sometimes as being too self-help like. But really, positive affirmations work. There are religions that base their entire system on positive prayer. Using positive affirmative words can greatly affect our energetic body.

Don't know any affirmations that you want to use? How about starting by reading through this list and see which one *feels* right for you. Try it out for a few days and see how your energetic body responds.

- Be still and know that I am God.
- I am happy. I am healthy. I am holy. (modified from a daily affirmation that James Van Praagh uses)
- I am safe and protected at all times
- Creativity flows through me with ease.
- I am powerful and strong. I can do anything I desire.
- I am love.
- It is safe for me to speak my truth.
- I am intuitive.
- My connection to the divine is strong and constant.

Vibrational Healing

Vibrational healing actually works on a pretty cool premise that make a lot of sense when you think about it. If you are into science, you may find this concept relates to your knowledge of how the world works. And if not, this is an easy way to explain energy to a friend that is a bit skeptical.

So, we know that everything is energy - everything is made of protons and electrons and all those science words you learned in high school. Now do you know that each of these protons and electrons is vibrating at a different frequency, some even popping in and out of existence without any known reason or pattern (at least not yet)?

Well each of your cells, made up of these protons and electrons, are also vibrating. Everything in this world is vibrating. The frequencies are just different. This table in front of me is vibrating at the frequency of a table. At its core, it is made of the exact same material as your cells - the same protons and electrons and little bits and pieces. The difference is that these little pieces are coming together all at the same frequency to make a table and the ones in your body are coming together to make a person.

Color Vibrations

Okay - now how can this knowledge help you on your path to health and healing? Remember how each of your chakras is associated with a certain color. The reason that this color is connected to the chakra is that they both vibrate at a similar frequency. So, to open and balance a chakra it helps to expose your cells to that vibrational frequency.

This whole method works similarly to tuning forks. When one tuning fork is hit the vibration of that fork will start to set off the other ones in its environment. This happens with other musical instruments as well such as drums. So just like the tuning fork, the more you are exposed to a certain vibrational frequency the more your body will start to vibrate at that frequency as well.

Practically, what does this look like? This could take the form of wearing more clothes that are in a certain color frequency range or even painting your fingernails in that color. Looking or being in an environment that is surrounded by a certain color will also influence the vibrational frequency of your chakras.

Sound Vibrations

And this isn't just color. Sound also has a frequency and listening to the frequencies that have been associated with chakras can help open that chakra. This is also why certain sounds are connected with each chakra and chanting that specific seed sound is believed to open the corresponding chakra. For example, chanting Om is thought to open and balance the crown chakra because their vibrational frequencies are similar.

I enjoy searching the internet for different compilations of sounds, finding what resonates with the chakra I am working on at any given time. Try this out and see what you think. Does listening to certain frequencies help your energetic body?

Crystal Vibrations

My favorite way to work with vibrational frequency healing is through the use of crystals. Some people think using crystals is junk science because they believe they can just hold a certain crystal for a few minutes and suddenly they will become lucky or have clairvoyant visions. This is not how crystals work.

Instead, crystals vibrate, just like you and that table, at certain frequencies. The more you are around the crystal and their frequency, the more you start to acclimate to that frequency. This is why it is best to choose just a few crystal energies to work with at one time, otherwise, you may overwhelm your body. It is also wise to keep the same few crystals for a length of time, giving your body enough time to resonate with the crystal.

Usually, you can find me with one crystal in each pocket and that is about all. I will keep these crystals with me throughout my day and at night I sleep with them right next to me. This gives my body the time to start to form a harmonic resonance with the crystal energies.

You can also accomplish this by meditating with the same crystal each day or wearing crystal jewelry. It also is nice to have a specific crystal dedicated to your nightstand to help with the vibrations of your bedroom.

Vibrations and the Aura

I talked in this section mainly relating to how the vibrational frequency affects the chakras, but this is also true with the aura. Using different vibrations can help cleanse the aura and draw out energy you do not want to be there.

I like to use black stones to draw out negative or harmful energies in an aura. For example, I sleep with a large piece of smokey quartz next to my bed so each night my aura can heal and cleanse itself. I recommend the dark colored crystals to remove and protect against negative energies and then the white or clear crystals to cleanse the aura.

If you know me and my family, you won't be surprised that I spend a lot of time going in and out of hospitals and doctor's clinics. Having a child with special needs means doctor's appointments every few weeks.

What people who are not energy sensitive sometimes do not realize, is that hospitals and clinics are full of the energies of fear and negativity. As an empath and someone sensitive to energy, I have to be very cautious when entering this type of environment so that I don't absorb and take on this type of energy. If I don't protect my energy, I can end up feeling tired and drained after only spending an hour in one of these places.

So, what do I do? I carry or wear dark crystals (usually black tourmaline) the day of an appointment. I have two small pieces, one for each pocket, that I like to carry on these days. Additionally, after the appointment is over I take a long cleansing shower (more on this later). Of course, sometimes this doesn't happen until late at night, but I make sure to incorporate it into my day. I will also then use a light-colored stone like selenite or clear quartz after the shower to cleanse and bring my energies back into balance. I do this with crystals, but you can use color, sound and other vibrational frequencies for this as well.

Specific Chakra Healing

Sometimes, what is really needed to get a chakra open and functioning correctly is a lifestyle change specific to that particular chakra. Nothing is going to get that root chakra open if its main issue is lack of physical exercise and you sit on the couch all day. That closed chakra may be telling you something about your lifestyle that you need to pay attention to.

So, what do you do about this? Look at the information surrounding each chakra and see where your lifestyle is lacking. That root chakra needs consistent sleep every night, a good diet and physical activity in addition to issues surrounding survival and security. Are you sleeping enough, eating good food and participating in moderate physical activity?

Now, look at your life - what areas are out of balance? Does this have any correlation to the chakras in your body that are not in balance? This may be the hardest method of all because it requires you to be honest with yourself and then do something about it. It is much easier to stay up all night long binge-watching Netflix on the couch then it is to get eight hours of sleep and wake up early to hit the gym. Sometimes there is no easy way out - you just have to put in the hard work.

Yoga

A method that is sometimes popular with energy healing is the use of yoga. Yoga and chakras seem to fit together pretty nicely and for some people, the first time they learn about the chakra system is during a yoga class. And there is a good reason for this - certain yoga poses will help to open different chakras as well as helping clear energy blocks from the aura.

Now I am not a certified yoga teacher so my knowledge on this is limited. What I do know is there are some awesome books out there on this subject that can start you on the path to healing.

You may also be lucky and find a great yoga teacher near you that can help you work on your specific energy situation - but just know that not all yoga teachers are created equal and not all of them have an advanced knowledge of the chakra and energy system.

You know who does have extensive knowledge of chakras and yoga? Anodea Judith. She has several books that are a great resource for individuals interested in this area as well as teaching workshops on this subject. If you want to use yoga to help balance your chakras I definitely recommend seeking out her work.

Meditation

Perhaps one of the best methods to balance your chakras and to cleanse your aura is through meditation and visualization. Here we need another brief science interlude.

Your thoughts, those things that come out of your head, they actually have a vibration to them and they go somewhere. And guess what - you can harness the power of those thoughts and those vibrations to help change the vibratory rate of your energy system. Pretty cool right. So how do you do this?

Cord Cutting

Cord cutting is a popular method used to heal your aura of energies that attach to it throughout your daily existence. We form energetic cords or connections to the people in our lives, to certain situations, to places even. Some of these cords are great, they help us to feel that love for our spouse or our children. But, other times, these cords attach to something not so nice - that ex-lover that you just want to get away from or that bad smoking habit that just won't quit.

These negative cords can then attach to our aura and sometimes to our energy centers. With these cords still attached, it becomes difficult for us to move on with our life or rid ourselves of bad habits. These cords can also show up as energy blocks or holes in our aura which can only be healed once those situations are removed.

So, now that we know we have these cords - how do we fix them? Cord cutting meditations are popular in the metaphysical community. There are a variety of different methods people use for this, but the best one is the one that works for you. Here are some options.

Some people like to call on an Archangel, such as Archangel Michael or Raphael and ask them to cut any negative cords that are attached to them. This is cool, and you should try it if it speaks to you, but not all people resonate with the concept of angels and sometimes it is best to take healing into your own hands. You do not need other entities help to heal yourself - you are capable of doing it yourself.

Another method is to go into a meditation and imagine yourself cutting the cords. This method empowers you and puts the tools in your own hands to take charge of your healing. Be aware though that sometimes it takes doing this several times over the course of a few weeks to finally get these cords to go away for good. Cords have a tendency to reattach themselves, even after our best effort.

There are many cord cutting meditations available for free on the internet. You can search around and find one that resonates with you. I have also included one in the Meditations section at the end of this book for you to try and see if you connect with it. Depending on the amount of work you do and the people you interact with, it may be a good idea to start a practice of incorporating a cord cutting meditation into your life at least once per week. I perform a small cord cutting exercise at the end of each client reading to make sure I am not keeping anything for myself.

Chakra Meditation

One of the most powerful ways to cleanse your chakras is through guided meditation. Visual meditations provide a powerful way to train your thoughts and your body to the feel what open and healthy chakras are like. In the Meditations section, you will find meditations for each individual chakra as well as a complete chakra cleansing meditation. These can be done separately or together. Try out these meditations and see how they make you feel. These can also work as examples for you to create your own meditation focusing on your specific needs and desires.

Closing Energetic Holes

The best way I have found to close up holes in the aura is also through meditation. There is a simple visualization exercise you can do that will start the healing process. With any kind of surgery, even a psychic one, it still takes time for the hole or wound to completely close. I have found that after doing this visualization the hole in the aura will slowly close up over the next one to two weeks.

To do this visualization simply see an image of yourself in your mind's eye. *Look* at your aura and see where the hole(s) are located. Then imagine you have a golden sewing needle and a spool of healing green thread. Take that thread and put it through the needle. Now take your golden needle of healing energy and sew up the hole you have found in your aura. You do not have to be an expert surgeon just do the best you can. After the hole is fully sewn shut take your hands and imagine healing loving energy is flowing out of them. Move your hands over this point in your aura and let the energy act as a salve protecting this location while it is closing up.

This is a relatively simple sounding "procedure" but if it is done with the proper intention it works beautifully to heal the auric field.

Shower Aura Cleanse

I love a good aura cleanse. And really, cleansing your aura can be pretty simple. There are many different methods, but most come down to envisioning yourself surrounded by a cleansing light. Perhaps my favorite method is to do an aura cleanse in the shower every morning. This way you start your day (or end it depending on when you bathe) with a clean and decluttered aura.

I believe I first heard about this method from the psychic medium John Edward. It is pretty simple and takes just a minute to do each day.

When you are in the shower use your shampoo and soap to scrub your hair and body. While doing this *see* all the gunk in your aura, those gray/black/brown/icky colors coming off and being released. Don't forget to do the palms of your hands and the bottoms of your feet (if it is safe). Then let the shower water wash away all this energetic dirt and see it going down the drain. Now that your energy is clean see a white light coming out of the shower head and covering your body. Let this white light permeate every cell and cleanse your energy.

See - pretty simple! Remember though, that as you go throughout your day your aura will continue to accumulate this energetic dirt. Just like there are dust particles that fly throughout the air barely seen there is also energetic clutter, remnants left behind, that you walk/roll/meander through every day.

I don't want to scare you or anything, this is nothing to worry about, you have been moving through this energetic clutter since you were born. You are likely used to it by now. If you are opening up and developing your psychic and intuitive skills, you may be more sensitive and notice this energetic debris more. A good protection technique can help lessen its effects and this shower aura cleanse can help clean your aura. Pretty simple!

Protective bubble

Now, if you want to avoid some of these energetic issues that come from just your daily existence, a good energetic protective practice is important. I felt I couldn't end this chapter without a simple protective meditation to help you along your path.

Using an energetic bubble of protection is one of the fundamental skills developing psychics, intuitive and energy workers learn. I have included my personal method in the Meditations section as well.

Saying that I am a visual person. The method you prefer should go along with your strengths. If you are a physical person, someone who works with their body and *feels* energy more than seeing it, it may be helpful to use your hands to create a bubble of energy by pushing your energy out to a point about arms distance from your body. Really feel a shield of energy around you and sense that your personal space and energy is surrounded by a hard shell.

If you are a visual person, work on *seeing* a bubble of white or blue light (or whatever light you see as protective) surrounding your body. See this bubble going above your head and below your feel. You can even see this bubble being filled with a reflective substance or a specific color of light that you want to work with.

If you are an auditory person, find a protective mantra that works for you and say it, either in your head or out loud, whenever you feel you need some protection.

As for my personal practice, it is something that has taken me years to refine and create. This is a practice that has evolved with me and that has changed when I needed it to change. I've taken bits and pieces of what I've learned over the years and morphed them into my own unique practice that I do every morning and throughout my day. I encourage you to use this as an example. Work on creating your own version using what works for you.

Energy Healing

Sometimes, you need to call in the big guns. Sometimes you need to go and see a professional energy healer. Believe me when I say that you are enough. You are enough to cleanse and heal your own body. You do not *need* anyone else to do this for you.

That said. Energy healers can be a great resource when you want that additional help or assistance in opening your chakras or clearing your energy. I like to give this suggestion with a heaping dose of caution. Make sure you find an energy healer that you trust. Someone that you get good vibes from and that appears legitimate. There are a great number of wonderful healers out there in the world. There are also a number of frauds. This is your energy - find someone that you trust to work on it.

My first introduction to energy healing was through a woman who was in a book group I had joined. She seemed to know what she was talking about and had training in an energy healing modality. However, after being around her for a while I determined she just didn't seem to have her life together. You know the type of person; her house was always a mess and she seems stressed out at every meeting. Even her physical body was actively rejecting food. Personally, I did not feel that this was an individual I wanted working with my energy. Energy is a sensitive and subtle matter. I want anyone who touches my energetic field and works with it to have a decent energy system themselves. But that is just my personal feeling, and you may have gotten a great vibe off this woman who possible would have helped you immensely. Trust your instincts here.

This woman from my book club practiced an energy modality I was not familiar with which goes to the point that there are a variety of different types of healers out there. Right now, as I write this, Reiki is a very popular modality of energy healing, but it is not the only one. There are a number of other energies available in the ethos for healers to use and that work. Research what is in your local area and find what you connect with. Also, know that some of these energies are available to be sent remotely, but, as I mentioned before, make sure you trust your healer.

Personally, I am Reiki II certified which means that I can give Reiki in person or at a distance, in space and time. I work with Reiki energy daily sending it to myself every morning. My other favorite energy to work with is one that I call "Love". It is this powerful love energy that I bring in from the essence of divinity and channel through my heart chakra and out through my hands. Both these energies have different *feelings* to them and different vibrations.

Find the energy system that you resonate with and a healer that can channel them. Trust your instincts and your intuition. Finding the right healer for you can be a process. Be patient with it.

Chakra and Aura Activities

Now that we have gone all through the energy systems - you know what chakras are and all about the aura. You know how to read your energy system and how to cleanse and balance it. Now that you have all this knowledge - how about we use it for something fun!

The one thing about all this information is that it will just be lost in a few weeks if you don't reinforce it and use it in some fashion. How much do you really remember from that high school algebra class anyway (unless of course, you are a math teacher)?

With this in mind, I've come up with a few activities you can do throughout your day to utilize this knowledge, so you don't forget it!

What Kind of Aura...

I love to play this game to reinforce the aura colors. I call it "what kind of Aura would you like..." It is simple really - if you could choose the aura of certain people what color would you pick? Think about the people you interact with on a daily basis. What auras and qualities of these colors would you like these people to have? Where do you want these colors in their energy system?

I've included some of the people I encounter below to give you an example of how I play this game along with a quick refresher on what the colors mean and why I chose them. Try it out for yourself and see what you think. Will you choose the same colors as me or something different?

Best Friend

If I were to choose the aura of my best friend, I would like this person to have a primarily pink aura with layers of orange and some yellow around their head. Pink is the color of love and individuals with this color tend to be very caring and nurturing - who couldn't use a friend like that! The orange would be for some creativity because it always helps to have a friend that comes up with new fun and exciting adventures to go on. Then the yellow for some intellect, I want a friend I can talk to. I wouldn't mind some indigo or blue in their aura either for some spiritual insight and intuition, but this would just be an extra layer.

Partner

Now partners are a different matter. Do you want your partner to have the same aura colors as your best friend or would you like something a bit different? Do you want someone who matches your aura, or do you prefer novelty?

One thing about partners, and anyone you spend a lot of time with is that you may find their auras starting to take on some of the same colors that are in your aura. Over time when we inhabit the same space with another individual their vibrational frequency will start to sync up with ours. This is why we feel so comfortable being around our family and where that feeling of "home" comes from.

So, what would your ideal partner's aura look like? I have myself a pretty great guy and his aura is different enough from mine to be unique but close enough in frequency to feel comfortable.

Kid's Teacher

If you could pick any teacher by their aura what would it look like? Since my little one is still in preschool I would like her teacher's aura to be primarily red so that she would have the energy to keep up with her young class. Some creative orange would also be helpful - maybe layered around her feet so that she would be more likely to come up with creative activities involving movement. Then I'd have to throw in some yellow around her head, because, even though this is just preschool, these young ones are still supposed to be learning. Finally, I would top it all off with a soft layer of pink to provide the hugs and comfort that my little girl needs.

What kind of aura would you like for your kid's teachers? Does it change depending on which kid you think about?

Spiritual teacher

What about a spiritual teacher? My ideal spiritual teacher looks very different than my ideal preschool teacher. I would like my spiritual teacher's aura to be primarily blue with a second layer of purple. Around their head, a layer of silver would also be nice.

I'm actually on the lookout for a good spiritual teacher, so if anyone of you knows someone with this aura combination can you send them my way (just kidding - well, only a little).

Doctor

Now I deal a lot with doctors since I am married to one and have a kiddo with special needs. And from my frequent interactions with them I can tell you - they are not all made the same. After being exposed to the number and variety that I have, I can definitely pick out my favorites quickly. But if I could pull up a list of doctors and search by their aura colors, now that would be amazing!

My ideal doctor would have an aura that is green. Green is the color of the healer and I want my doctor to be focused on health. I would also like some indigo around the doctor's head because although they don't like to admit it, a lot of medicine isn't really based on science it is based on intuition. I want this doctor to follow any "gut instincts" they have - even if they don't realize what those instincts really are. Finally, I would like a layer of pink around this doctor's body to provide that warm reassurance needed.

Barista

Who loves a good barista? What kind of aura would you like that person mixing your latte to have? You know what - my barista would have very similar color combinations as that of my ideal preschool teacher - maybe switch the orange and red color positions. Hmmm, how about that - I would never have thought that my ideal barista would be a preschool teacher...

What about you, what would your ideal aura look like for the various categories. What category did I leave out that interests you?

Painting Rooms

Have you ever walked into a room and felt your energy change dramatically? Did a calm sweep over you or did you get antsy and uneasy? What do you think caused this shift? Anything in common with these experiences?

How about this - what color were these rooms? Did the color directly or indirectly influence your emotions or what you were feeling?

For most of us, our world is full of many different colors. What we don't always realize, and sometimes take for granted, is the impact that these colors have on us throughout the day. Sit all day in a room painted a light shade of blue and I'm betting you will be a lot calmer than sitting in a bright red room.

With this in mind, how about we play another game! In this one, you imagine what color you would like each of the rooms in your living space to be painted and pair it with what chakra you would like to activate.

Let's start with the kitchen. This is a place where food is stored and prepared for your family members. What color is your kitchen now? What color would you like it to be? Do you want to be more creative and activate your sacral chakra with your culinary inspirations - maybe some orange is in order? Or maybe you want to serve your family food that is healing and full of love, how about a green kitchen to work on that heart chakra.

Think of what impact you want for your kitchen and which color choice you would choose.

Now move into your living room. How do you want people to feel when you entertain them? How do you want to feel after a long day, which chakras do you want to activate? Which colors accomplish these goals?

Now, imagine that you were in one room for hours on end without the ability to leave of your own free will. What color would you want that room to be? How would you want that room to make you feel? Now think about if you were the one choosing that color for another person. That is exactly what parents do every day when they pick out nursery colors and decorate their children's rooms. What color and associated chakras do you want to activate for your children (or pets)?

Let's move next to your bedroom. Do you want your bedroom to be a relaxing oasis or do you prefer something a little more active?

Are you starting to see how colors can play a large role in our environment and in helping our chakra systems? But also remember that you do not need to paint an entire room a new color to get those color benefits. You can also add decorative detail to that room. So how about those throw pillows and blanket in the living room. What color are they? And what if you want your kitchen to be creative and healing - how about olive green walls with some orange kitchen towels?

Now it is time for you to have some fun. Can you redecorate your home in your head to make each room ideal? What accents would you like to add to put that pop of color in each room? After you finish your living space take on your family members and friends. Then move onto office buildings and places you go every day. This game can keep going and going. Now just be careful that you don't spend a fortune redecorating your entire house!

The Story of You

Delving into the world of your energetic body you likely have had some revelations. You know by now that when exploring these systems, you have to be honest with yourself. You may learn things that you like, and some things that you are not very happy about.

Maybe you realize that the black spot in your aura is a block and when you look more into it you discover it is coming from a negative cord attached to an ex-boyfriend you told yourself you were over. Perhaps that throat chakra is closed and blocked, and now you have to admit to yourself that you are not speaking your truth, especially at work. You realize that you need to really speak up for yourself in order for that throat chakra to finally open up.

For this activity I want you to write out every color in your aura and the state of every chakra. Next to this write what this says about you and what you can do to heal it if it needs healing. Really take the time to examine yourself under a lens, looking closely at all the different aspects of yourself you have discovered.

I find that this activity works best in written form. It is easy to just think about all these things, but when you see them in front of you in writing it becomes a more concrete reality.

I know, this can be scary, but guess what? I will do it here myself for you so that you can see what I'm talking about. So that you can see the honesty and truth needed to really make a change and difference in your world.

The Colors in My Aura

I'll start out with the colors in my aura. Over the course of the last year, my aura has changed and expanded greatly. There are a lot of new colors that have come into my energetic body that were not there a year ago. In the past, my aura was primarily blue and indigo. You will see that, due to the work I have been undertaking, my aura contains many different hues now.

Blue: This is the main color in my aura and has been present for a long time. It does not surprise me that this is the primary color and I am glad that it is in my aura. I like the feel of the color and it feels like home to me.

Indigo: This is the secondary color in my aura and is also located throughout my auric field. I am proud that this color is present as I spent a long time working on and developing my intuition and psychic abilities. I still remember reading books on how to be a psychic and feeling disappointed that I didn't feel like I was making any progress. This indigo is a sign that when I put in the effort the reward will show up, it just may take some time.

Green: This green started to appear in my aura about six months after I became attuned to Reiki. I never thought of myself as a healer, but when this color started to appear I understood that healing can come in many forms.

Silver: To be honest, I was surprised when this color started to appear in my aura. I checked my aura daily for about a week as this color made its appearance. It started around my head and then descended throughout my aura. The day before it appeared for the first time my aura was totally grey. This worried me at first, but then I saw the next day the grey was gone, and silver appeared.

Gold: The gold came about a month after the silver appeared. It had the same process of appearing. A day of grey totally enveloping my aura and then the gold appeared around my head and gradually moved to surround my whole aura. I still do not have a total understanding of why my aura has gold in it. I do not *think* I communicate with our deceased loved ones regularly, but I may be having experiences that I just do not realize are related to this.

Orange: The orange in my aura started to show up when I began writing this book. I enjoyed having it there and it feels very familiar to me. Like a color that has been there before and is like an old friend.

Purple: Like the gold, I was surprised when the purple appeared in my aura. And just like the gold, I do not totally understand its presence. I do focus heavily on the spiritual world and spreading my knowledge to others, so I am guessing this is the reason it is here.

Grey and Black: I have grey around my right wrist with a concentration of black in the center of it. This is an old injury that I received when I followed a path I was not meant to go down. After I graduated law school I always said I would not take the bar exam because I didn't want to be a "real" lawyer. I knew that wasn't the path for me and not taking the bar exam was my minor stand against the inevitable. But, as usually happens when you don't stick with your intuitive insights, I went back on my ideals and agreed to take the exam and ended up working as a lawyer. While studying for the big test I developed a sore wrist, likely from overuse. Energetically it was from following a path that was not meant to be and that I knew deep down did not fit who I was. So this injury acts up from time to time, reminding me of who I am and what my purpose is in this lifetime.

Hole: As previously mentioned, I have a hole in my aura over my heart chakra in the front of my body. I believe this is due to perpetually shutting down my heart chakra. I know of its existence and have used the psychic surgery meditation to repair it previously. This works but I seem to re-tear open the hole when I am not careful - I guess I need to do the meditation again!

The State of my Chakras

So, this section is going to be a little boring as, at this moment right now, all my chakras are open and balanced, including my transpersonal chakras. However, I will write as if my heart and root chakras are closed because this is a common state that I regularly experienced before becoming deeply acquainted and working with my energy system.

Root Chakra: Closed and Blocked - my root chakra likes to close on me when I succumb to fear. This is the kind of fear that includes being afraid of bumps in the night and ghost stories. This fear is not always rational. I know that because this fear will lead to closing my root chakra that I need to be hyperaware of what I watch and the books I read. Scary ghost stories are a no go for me. If I watch something violent I know that I am going to need to pay attention to my energy system and take the steps needed to keep my root chakra open. I am also working with myself constantly to be honest and figure out where this fear actually stems from. I believe it is based on a fear of the unknown, so I try to educate myself on the paranormal world, taking care not to scare myself, so that the unknown will become known.

Sacral Chakra: Open and Blocked - see how that root chakra being closed will block my other chakras? My sacral chakra is usually open and my creativity flowing.

Solar Plexus Chakra: Open and Blocked - I am proud that this chakra is opened as I used to have a lot of issues stemming from self-worth - I mean, what teenage girl doesn't? But I gained the confidence over the years to trust myself and who I am. I spent a long time denying the essence of me, but now I am doing what I love and being myself. This chakra is healthy and shining!

Heart Chakra: Closed and Blocked - this chakra closes a lot to prevent me from feeling too much. Being an empath, I feel more than other people, specifically those emotions of other individuals that I am around. What does this really mean? This means that if someone next to me in yoga class is having some anxiety I am going to feel that anxiety. To prevent this, I used to close this heart chakra so the emotions were not as strong. Now that I know that I do this I work on finding different ways to protect myself energetically instead of closing my heart chakra.

Throat Chakra: Open and Blocked - this is another chakra that I am proud to have opened. I am a quiet person and sometimes have a difficult time speaking up for what I believe. I have worked hard to gain the confidence in the solar plexus that has allowed me to speak my truth.

Third Eye Chakra: Open and Blocked - see how that root chakra being closed affects all my chakras, even the ones that usually are functioning pretty well? This shows how important it is to focus on all your chakras and not just the ones that interest you.

Crown Chakra: Open and Blocked - my crown chakra usually functions nicely. I cultivate my relationship with the divine in a daily and weekly practice. I pray and talk to my spirit guides every day. I attend church each week. I perform full moon and new moon rituals when I feel the need. All of this is to say that I have a strong and positive connection to the divine.

Whew - so that is my energetic body, all laid out and exposed for you to see! Now it is your turn. What does your energetic body look like? What do you feel about its appearance?

Conclusion

Thank you for taking this journey with me through the energetic body. I hope you have learned a little about yourself along the way. Use the tools that I have provided you to help create the life you want to live.

I also recommend reading from a lot of different sources and trying out the different methods from various authors. We all have our own opinions and experiences. Take what works from these sources and start to create your own ideas and systems.

I hope you realize that you have the power within yourself to heal your energetic body. You decide through your thoughts and actions what takes place in your life. There may be destiny points and situations that are out of your control, but you have the power to determine how you respond to these occurrences.

I have learned a lot about myself and my own energy body by studying and looking at the energy systems of other individuals. This is a process that has taken me years to get to. This is not something that happened overnight. Do not give up if you don't see an aura the first time or if you can't feel the difference in the states of your chakras. Practice. Try. Take some time each day to work on a method that interests you. You will find, eventually, you can do what you desire.

It took me years to see colors in auras. Five years to be exact. This is something that I worked on and off with consistently. I would spend a few minutes each time I took a shower trying to see the colors in my aura around my hands and feet. Gradually my eyes developed this ability. I would work on seeing the minister's aura during church service. The aura of the trees as I was walking my dog. It is a process. It takes time.

The energy system is subtle but extensive. I know that you will be able to learn and practice every technique that you want to. I believe in you. You are a child of the divine and are worthy of all the success you desire.

Meditations

I recommend reading through these meditations first before trying them out. Some people like to record them and listen back or have someone read it to you. You can also just remember the general themes of the meditations and proceed on your own. Relax - breathe deeply - and let your intuition flow.

Cord cutting meditation

Take a deep breath. And now another. And another. See your body standing in a beautiful white room. The energy in this room is healing and palpable, filled with love and light. Take a breath and step out of your body so that you can see it right in front of you. Look at your body up and down, starting with the head and moving all the way to the feet.

Focus on any areas that seem to have cords of energy coming out of them. Do these cords look healthy and bright or are they muddied and diseased? Find any cords that do not look healthy. Note where they are and how they look.

Now, ask your guides or higher self to provide you with the tool needed to cut these cords. Look in your hand and see what appears. It may be a pair of scissors. It may be a knife or a sword. This item may change each time you do this meditation or stay the same. Trust what your guides have given you.

Now take the tool and go to the first unhealthy cord you see. Cut that cord off your body. Now, in your dominant hand (right for most people) see a glowing light of green and white energy start to flow out. Place this hand over the cord end that you just cut off. Send, with the intention love and healing, energy to the person, place or thing attached to the other end of the cord.

After you have sent the healing energy, look at the spot where the cord was connected to you. Take your fingers or ask your guides for a tool to remove any remnants of the cord that still remain stuck in this location. Do they give you tweezers or just suggest you use your fingers? Once all the cord particles have been removed, imagine once again that healing light flowing out of your dominant hand. This time place it over the location where the cord was just removed. See that location healing up and the entry point for the cord closing. See it glowing with love and light.

Repeat these steps for any remaining cords you find. Take your time and be patient with the process. There is no reason to rush. You can always come back and heal any remaining cords at a later date.

Once all the cords have been removed and love sent in both directions, see the white light of the room around you start to pulsate. Feel the love that is in the room coming closer to you until it engulfs you in a warm hug. Let this loving energy course throughout your body, cleansing any negativity or doubt that it finds.

Take a deep breath. Move back into your body. Take another breath. And another. Start to find yourself back in the present moment. In the present time. Take a breath and breathe in the love that is your birthright.

Meditations for each chakra

Root Chakra Meditation

Take a deep breath. And another. And another. Imagine that you are in a room filled with red walls. The furniture in this room is red. The decorations are all different shades of red. This room vibrates at the frequency of red. Find the chair that looks the most comfortable and sit in it. Take a deep breath and just relax.

If you feel tired let yourself doze off a little. Feel your body melting into the chair. Now feel roots start to grow out of your feet into the earth, anchoring you to this place. Here you feel safe and secure. You feel protected. You can just let go and relax.

Now take an internal scan of your root chakra. How does it look? What direction is it moving in? Does it have any spots or fuzzy areas? Do not judge the state of the chakra just note what it looks like.

Right in front of you, there appears a fine mist of red air. Breathe this red air in and see it going to that root chakra. See that red air mixing with the energy of your root chakra and cleaning it of any smudges or stains. Keep breathing in this red energy and see it assisting your root chakra in opening up and spinning beautifully. Your root chakra starts to have a brilliant red color as it spins itself open.

Take a moment and just enjoy this feeling. You are safe. You are protected. You have everything you need right here. Your root chakra is open and shining brightly.

Take a breath and come back into yourself. Become aware of the current time and space. Take another breath. You are safe.

Sacral Chakra Meditation

Breathe in. Breathe out. Repeat again. And again. Imagine a dance floor opens up in front of you. A spotlight shines in the center. You know that light is for you. This time is for you. Someone appears out of the shadow and walks to the middle of the spotlight. You know it is your guide - here to lead you in life and in dance.

You walk forward. Music starts to play in the background. You can hear the vibrations. You can feel the vibrations. Your hips start to sway as you approach your guide - your partner.

Take your partner's hand. Let your guide lead you in this dance. Feel your body moving to the vibrations of the music. Feel the music pulse through you. Heat rises from your feet and settles in your pelvis, accentuating your dance moves. Feel the rhythm. Feel the heat.

The song slowly ends, and you feel your body still pulsing from the movement. Take a breath. Come back into yourself. Take another breath. You are back in the room, back in your body and the present time - but the melody of the song still remains with you. You feel a sense of openness with the world before you.

Listen to that melody when it shows up in your life. Know that this is a sign that you need to dance to your music. To let go and feel the creativity flow through you.

Solar Plexus Chakra Meditation

Take a breath. And another. And another. Feel the warm summer sun pour down all around you. Feel it entering your body and warming you to the core. Here you feel safe. You feel secure.

Now see yourself back in school. You are sitting at your desk and the teacher is handing back papers. You sit there waiting to see what grade you received. As she comes by your desk she drops your paper in front of you. You look at the grade. In a bright yellow marker, it says A+.

A rush of excitement goes through you. You look at the title of the paper. The title reflects the area in your life you are currently struggling with. It could be "How I found Mr. Right" or "The Perfect Career" or "How to interact with my boss while staying confident". What is the title of your paper?

Smile and know that you have all the knowledge and ability in any given field or task. Feel the confidence in yourself. It is there always waiting to be acknowledged and received. You can do anything you want to do. You are a child of the divine and in such you are the essence of divinity.

Take a deep breath. And another. Come back to your body and the room you are in. Know in your gut that you are worthy of anything and everything.

Heart Chakra Meditation

Take a deep breath. And another. And another. Suddenly you find yourself walking down a beautiful path. There are tall trees filled with green leaves on each side and the golden sun is glistening through the branches. The sound of birds chirping can be heard in the distance and the rattle of a branch as a squirrel runs across can be heard up above.

This place feels safe. It feels like home. As you walk down this path you find yourself in a clearing. Go towards it. Here there is a little ledge that looks over a gentle pond. Find a comfortable spot and sit down here, overlooking the beautiful water.

There is something about this place - a sense of love starts to fill the air. You can see the air right in front of you turn a beautiful shade of emerald green. Breathe in this air and see it go to your heart center filling your chest. This air smells so pure and clean that you take in another breath and another.

The green air now fills your entire body as you continue to breathe it in. Your exhales turn green and soon this green air is floating all around you. You can feel your heart center start to pulsate with this light, coming alive and beating strong. Take this energy of love and use your heart center to push the energy out into the world. See it going towards your loved ones and encompassing them. See it going to your neighborhood, your community, your country. This green energy of love moves through space and time to any situation that has wronged you, anything and anywhere love is needed. Send this energy out into the universe. To all of creation.

Now send this energy to yourself. Know in your heart of hearts that you deserve this love just as much as those you send it to. You are made of the same divine essence as the heavens and the earth. You deserve the love that is your birthright.

Take a breath. And another. And another. Come back to your body, your room and know that you are loved. You are love.

Throat Chakra Meditation

Take a deep breath. And another. And another. Feel the air flowing through your throat on its way down to your lungs. Feel the air as it comes back up. Notice any changes in the air. Is it warmer on the way out? Is it easier to feel in one direction as opposed to the other?

Establish a gentle rhythm, in and out, in and out, feeling the air as it makes its way down your throat and back up again. Keep at this rhythm and pace.

Now see yourself, in your mind's eye on a stage. The lights are shining brightly on you and you cannot see who is in the audience in front of you. Behind you, beautiful blue velvet curtains are shut tight. Two feet in front of you stands a lone microphone. Step towards it.

In this microphone announce to the audience and the world everything that has been on your mind and that you have kept in, kept unsaid. Tell your boss what you really think of him. Tell your neighbor's kid where he can put that soccer ball. Let loose on everything that you have held back.

Feel a sense of relief sweep over you. A sense of lightness. But it isn't over yet. The sound of instruments tuning can be heard behind you and the blue velvet curtains open to reveal a band. Your own personal band. A song instantly springs to your mind and the band knows right away what cords to play.

Here you are on stage, a stage built just for you with a band here just for you. Belt out that song. You hear your voice leaving you and it sounds perfectly tuned and on pitch. Every note you sing is the right one. You finish the song and the audience in front of you stands - clapping and cheering your name.

Take a breath. And another. And another. Return to your body. Feel that throat chakra alive and humming its own tune.

Third Eye Chakra Meditation

Take a deep breath. In and out. Take another breath. And another. We are now going to work on creating a room for you. This is a place you can go to anytime when you want to get in touch with your third eye center and work on straightening and developing it.

In front of you picture a door. Note how the door looks. Is it big, is it small? What color is this door? What does its handle look like? Does it have any discernible features? This door leads to your private space. A space only you can go to and only those who you say can have access.

Open this door. Take a pause as you survey what lays inside. Now step inside and shut the door behind you. Look at your room. Notice the color of the walls, the floor, the furniture. Notice any knickknacks or doodads that are on tables and bookshelves. This room is filled with items that symbolize you and your work in this place.

Now walk over to one of the chairs you see. Sit down in this chair. To one side is a remote. Pick up this remote and you will see that it has all the colors of the chakras on it. Simply by pressing each colored button, you are able to open your chakras.

Start with the red button on the bottom and press it. Feel the energy in the room move into your root chakra. Now continue to press the buttons in order and feel the energy move up through your chakra system. Orange - Yellow - Green - Blue - Indigo - Purple.

As the energy rises you see a screen appear right in front of you. This is your psychic movie screen. On it, the images and scenes from your third eye center will play for you.

With all your chakras opened and functioning and your screen in place, sit back and watch. First, on the screen, a cute dog appears. He is white with brown spots. He sits there panting and wagging his tail expectantly. Now, think a color in your head and watch the dog shift to that color. What color dog is now sitting on the screen in front of you?

The dog wanders off the screen and now you see the image of a square. Next to the square are other shapes - a circle, triangle, oval, star. You realize this is a game. Using the power of your mind you move each of the shapes inside the square. First the circle, then the triangle, then the oval inside the triangle and finally the star. Once completed, the game disappears off the screen.

Now on your screen, a smiling face appears. This is a signal for the next exercise to begin. In your mind say the emotion "joy" and see what image appears. Pay attention and remember this image. Next, say the emotion "sadness" and see what image appears. Now "excitement". And "heartache". Know that these are the symbols and pictures that your guides will use for you when they are communicating these emotions to you.

Look once more around your room. Know that this is your safe place. You can come here anytime you want to practice these or other third eye exercises. Rise from your seat and move to the door. Open the door and see yourself sitting in front of you.

Return to your body and take a breath. And another. Breathe in the cool air in front of you. Now smile knowing that you now have a secret place you can go to anytime you want. Your psychic room.

Crown Chakra Meditation

Take a deep breath. And another. Feel the air coming in through your nose and watch it as it flows out. Take a breath in through your nose counting to four. Hold it for four pauses. Now out through your mouth for a count of four. Let's repeat this - in through your nose - hold - out through your mouth. And again.

In front of you, there is a swirling tornado of purple light. You can see little specks of white glistening in this light. Take a breath and step into this swirling energy.

Inside the vortex, you feel safe and comforted. An overwhelming feeling of love and support washes through you. Your whole body starts to tingle and feel alive.

Take a step through the tornado and you find yourself on top of a brilliant white cloud. In front of you, there are two white chairs. You move towards the one closest to you and sit down. Take a breath and just enjoy the beautiful location you are in and the sense of awe and wonder that surrounds you.

As you sit in this chair you see a beautiful light in the distance. It slowly moves closer and closer to you. As it nears you see that this light takes the shape of a person. The energy of love flowing off this individual is divine.

This person comes closer and takes a seat in the chair across from yours. You instantly recognize this individual as one of your spirit guides. Notice their features. Do you feel anything in particular? Smell anything? Sense anything?

Now is your time to ask this guide any questions you may have. Listen with your heart for the response. Take as long as you need or want with your guide, always knowing that you can come back to this place whenever you need to.

The swirling purple energy tornado appears again. You thank your guide and send them love as you get up and move towards this purple energy. You step into the light and are transported back to the present time. The present place.

Take a breath. And another. And another. Know that your guide is always with you, no matter where you are. You can always call on their loving and divine presence.

Full Chakra cleaning and spinning meditation

Take a breath. And another. And another. Feel the air coming in and filling your lungs. Then feel it leave. Take another breath.

You find yourself in a brilliant white room. Here you can see your physical and energetic bodies. Take a step outside your body and look at it fully. Notice your chakras and any characteristics they may have. Are they moving? Which direction? What color are they? Are there any splotches or dark spots?

You look to your right and a vacuum cleaner appears. It has a long hose on it with any attachment you feel you might need. Take this vacuum hose and go towards your body.

First, starting at the root chakra look for any dark or dusty spots. Use your divine vacuum cleaner to clear off any of these areas that look dirty. Now move next to your sacral chakra - then to your solar plexus - your heart chakra - your throat chakra - your third eye chakra - your crown chakra.

Take your time, making sure all the dark spots are gone. Returning to any spaces you feel are still dirty.

Now take the vacuum hose and place it at the top of your head on your crown chakra. Let it suck up any negativity, any energetic dust and dirt that isn't associated with your main chakras.

Once complete turn off your vacuum cleaner and take a look at your work. Notice how there are no longer any dark spots on your chakras.

Next, see seven cups appear in front of you. Each has a different color of energetic liquid corresponding to the chakras. Start with the red cup. Take the energetic liquid and pour it into your root chakra. See your root chakra becoming a brilliant red color. As you continue to pour the liquid your root chakra opens up and you can see it spinning beautifully. The liquid works as a fuel, energizing the chakra.

With your root chakra a brilliant red color, put down the cup and take the orange cup next. Each cup has exactly the right amount of energetic liquid in it for each of your chakras. Pour the orange on your sacral chakra and see it turning a brilliant shade and spinning beautifully.

Repeat this step with the remaining cups. The yellow for the solar plexus - the green for the heart chakra - the blue for the throat chakra - the indigo for the third eye chakra - and the purple for the crown chakra.

Take your time with each color. Watch as your chakras start to glow in beautiful brilliant light. Once completed take a step back and admire your work.

Now a large cup of sparkling energetic liquid appears. It is the color of brilliant diamonds. Take this liquid and pour it over the top of your energetic body. Watch as it descends through your body adding sparkle and shine to each chakra. This diamond energy also moves around your body covering your auric field. Cleansing each spot as it goes.

Look at the brilliant site before your eyes. Your energy centers are clear, powerful and full of love and light. Know that you can repeat this process whenever you need to.

Step back inside this brilliant body and take a breath. And another. And another. Come back to your present time and place. Feel the sense of renewal and energy that is coursing through you.

My Personal Daily Meditation

Breathe in. Breathe out. Breathe in. Breathe out. Breathe in. Breathe out. Sense the energy above you, high up in the ethers. The energy of divinity. Bring that energy down. Feel it, see it coming in through your head and going through your body, out through your feet and deep into the earth until it touches the earth's core. Now feel the energy rising back up through the layers of the earth, this grounding protective energy.

Feel it coming up in through your feet, your legs and into your first chakra. The root chakra. Breathe the color red into this chakra and feel the energy expand. Next move up to your sacral chakra. Feel the energy spinning. Breathe the color orange into this energy center. Now feel the energy rise to your solar plexus chakra. Breathe in the color yellow. See the chakra energizing and taking on that bright yellow color. Bring the energy up to your heart chakra. Breathe in the color green. Feel the chakra expanding and opening up. Now feel the energy move up to your throat chakra. Breathe in blue. Move it up to your third eye chakra. Breathe in indigo and see the chakra opening and expanding. Now move your energy up to your crown chakra. Breathe in purple. Feel the energy expanding beyond the crown of your head and upward. First white, then gold, then sparkling diamond, and finally up into the essence.

Bring that energy of divinity back down through your body again, this time saying, "The light of God flows through me." Now imagine a blanket of divinity being draped over your shoulders while saying "The love of God enfolds me" - feel the love that surrounds you on all sides. Now imagine a vertical circle surrounding your aura and see it moving around your body three times to encircle your aura in a sphere of protective light (I see this light as a blue matrix of protective light but use the color that works for you). Say "The power of God protects me". While in this energy bubble see your guides and angels appear. I see one angel in each direction, one standing in front of my energy bubble, one behind and one on each side. Then I see my protective animal guides standing next to the angels at my sides (my protective animals are lions that will sometimes sit still and other times they circle my energy bubble). While seeing this say, "The presence of God watches over me". Now see yourself in your protective bubble with all the protective entities surrounding you. See the people in your life that you will encounter in the day ahead with the light of divinity shining through them. Say "Wherever I am God is and all is well".

A Note on the Prayer for Protection

I use a modified version of Unity Church's Prayer for Protection written by James Dillet Freeman. I encourage you to use whatever prayer or words work best for you. It may be the Lord's prayer or a poem you create yourself. It can even be a spell of protection. I personally resonate with the Unity Church and their prayer for protection, so I use this in my meditation. If this does not resonate with you do not use it.

The correct words of the prayer are:
The light of God surrounds us;
The love of God enfolds us;
The power of God protects us;
The presence of God watches over us;
     Wherever we are, God is!

ABOUT THE AUTHOR

Mary Shannon is an intuitive counselor who works with clients from around the world. Her ultimate goal is to help each individual see the light within themselves and to direct them back to their soul's purpose for coming to this earth. Knowing that the whole metaphysical field can sometimes seem pretty wacky and even scary, she strives to help normalize the field - to bring it out of the spooky realm and show that it is actually a practical and helpful tool. For more information or to book a reading, visit her website at *sevencupsmystic.com*.

Made in the USA
Columbia, SC
22 February 2018